GLORY TODAY FOR CONQUEST
TOMORROW

OTHER BOOKS BY ROBERT G. LEE:

Lord, I Believe
From Feet to Fathoms
Beds of Pearls
Whirlwinds of God
A Greater Than Solomon
The Grand Canyon of Resurrection Realities
The Name Above Every Name
The Blood of Jesus Christ
Pickings
Lee Lines
Proximities of Calvary

Glory Today
for Conquest Tomorrow

SIGNIFICANT SERMONS

by
ROBERT G. LEE, D.D., LL.D., Litt.D.
Pastor, Bellevue Baptist Church
Memphis, Tennessee

ZONDERVAN PUBLISHING HOUSE
GRAND RAPIDS, MICHIGAN

DEDICATION

To my daughter —

MRS. E. R. KING — Child of my love and prayer,

and

To my little granddaughter —

BETTY LEE KING, "sweet as the twilight notes
of the thrush,"

This volume is gratefully dedicated

by

THE AUTHOR

CONTENTS

CHAPTER ONE

GLORY TODAY FOR CONQUEST TOMORROW

And was transfigured before them: and his face did shine as the sun, and his raiment was white as the light.—MATT. 17:2

IN THE BIBLE, book above and beyond all books as a river is beyond a rill in reach, there are three accounts of the transfiguration event in the life of our Lord Jesus. Matthew, with the care of one who plants precious seed, tells of His transfiguration when the inner light of Christ's deity suddenly burst through His flesh and put an awe-inspiring radiance upon His brow. Mark, with the enthusiasm of one who has seen hidden glories revealed, writes of the wonder of that transcendent hour when Jesus was "metamorphosed before three." Luke, with the earnestness of one who puts a silver trumpet to his lips to summon people to worship, writes of that beautiful scene in the holy mount — a scene which was a pattern of the kingdom yet to come in power, even as the Tabernacle was a pattern of heavenly things.

For we have not followed cunningly devised fables, when we made known unto you the power and coming of our Lord Jesus Christ, but were eyewitnesses of his majesty. For he received from God the Father

> *honor and glory, when there came such a voice to him from the excellent glory, This is my beloved Son, in whom I am well pleased. And this voice which came from heaven we heard, when we were with him in the holy mount.*—II PETER 1: 16-18

And of this event when, as Jesus prayed, His manhood bloomed with deity, we do speak now:

I — THE TAKING — *"Jesus* TAKETH *Peter, James, and John into a high mountain apart."*

Always was Jesus taking those men — those three of the inner circle — somewhere. Always He had these three mighties whom He allowed to accompany Him in some of the most sacred, intimate, and epochal hours of His ministry. With Him were these three men, witnesses of His power, at the raising of the little daughter of Jairus (Mark 5:37). With Him were these three men, flesh-wearied sleepers, during His agony in the garden of Gethsemane, when the roots of His divine emotion put forth their crimson tears. With Him were these three men, sore-afraid witnesses of His glory in the mountain, when, by His person "suddenly changed with enhanced effulgence," He confirmed His precious utterances about His deity — the utterances which He had allowed them to ponder and meditate upon for six days.

"He taketh them apart"—up on the top of old Mount Hermon, nearly ten thousand feet high, wearing its mantle of snow by day and by night, wearing its turban of light by day. What blessedness for Jesus, for solitude had much to do with His earthly life. Keeping Himself fresh by union with unseen and unfailing springs, He was ever in touch with God. Divinely proficient in the art of isolating the inner life, He kept His outer life pungent and profound.

But, I reverently venture to say, the sweetest blessedness of this taking them apart into this high mountain was the high and holy privilege devoutly to be desired and attained — this privilege of having a part in bringing high hours of spiritual experience and joy and instruction to people — like a physicist who visualizes the invisible and glorifies the obscure, like a Gospel tailor who rustles divine garments in human ears, like a bugler who stirs human hearts to gratitude by the silver trumpets of testimony, like an astronomer who brings distant worlds near. I am sure that it was with joy and with a divine sense of His opportunity that Jesus took these men "into a high mountain apart."

However, we emphasize what a high privilege and blessedness was theirs — this chance to be alone with Him. It is ever a great experience to be alone with great men. Blessed experience if I, if you, could have been alone with General Diaz, when, after the defeat of the Austrians at the Piave River, he said "Deus Fecit." Blessed experience if I, if you, could have been in a lonely place apart with Judson, with Livingstone, when they lit gospel lamps in foreign lands. Blessed experience if you, if I, could have been with Carey when, on the day the French revolutionists tore the cross from Notre Dame, he landed at Calcutta and claimed a continent for Christ. Blessed experience if you, if I, had been alone with Paton the day he heard the first man amid thousands of cannibals speak in faith the name "Jesus." Blessed experience if you, if I, could have been alone that day with Willis Hotchkiss when, after two and a half years' work, he found the word for "Savior" in the language of the African tribe. Blessed experience if you, if I, could have heard Galileo when he found out that the earth goes around the sun. Blessed experience if I, if you, could have stood alone on the deck of the little ship with Columbus as a new world came in sight. Blessed experience if I, if you, had heard the sound of the hammer that became as claps of thunder circling the world as Luther nailed the theses to the church door at Wittenberg. Blessed experience if I, if you, had been alone with Oliver Cromwell when he stretched, for the first time, a psalm into a war drum. Blessed experience if you, if I, could have been alone with Lee as, refusing the leadership of the Northern armies offered him by Abraham Lincoln, he turned from Arlington and rode away. Blessed experience if you, if I, could have been beside Lincoln as he breathed his last and Seward said, "Now he belongs to the ages." Blessed experience, if you, if I, had been alone with Jackson as he prayed in his tent before a battle. Blessed experience if you, if I, had been alone with George Washington as he prayed in the snows at Valley Forge. Blessed experience if you, if I, had been with the pilgrims as they landed in New England, with Bunyan in jail, with Paul in Rome. But, oh, to have been "in a high mountain apart with Jesus" as were Peter, James and John at His transfiguration!

But still we can know the blessedness of aloneness, of apartness, with Christ whose face never lost its light, whose words never weakened in their authority, whose hands never failed in their tenderness, whose faculties never knew impoverishment or defeat, whose heart never lost its compassion, because He knew how to withdraw into solitude and to take others into the solitude with Him, showing us that one cannot set and serve a lavish table from a pantry poorly replenished. We can have high hours apart with Him in the kitchen, in the office, in the rush of business matters, and even in the crowds — if we have ears keenly sensitized to hear His voice. Still we can, following His beckoning, yielding to His leadership, which is both leadership and comradeship, find high mountains apart in our homes and the closets thereof.

God said to Elijah, "Hide thyself." And then, after the hiding, He said, "Show thyself." All of which means that God would have us to go into the silence— to fill up, to generate power, before we try to impart power, to suspend life for a while, to sit and wait the disclosure of God's plans and purposes. This means, too, that we ought to see the face of God before we see the face of man. Enter into the closet with God before we enter the conflict for God. Go into the private place *with* God before we enter the public place *for* God. How true it is that

> If chosen men had never been alone,
> In deep mid-silence, open-doored to God,
> No greatness ever had been dreamed or done.

John Oxenham speaks of it in these words:

> A little place of mystic grace,
> Of self and sin swept bare,
> Where I may look upon Thy face,
> And talk with Thee in prayer.

II — THE TRANSFIGURATION — "*And he was transfigured before them.*"

Matthew says: "His face did shine as the sun, and his raiment was white as the light." Mark says: "And his raiment became shining, exceeding white as snow, so as no fuller on earth can white them."

Nothing less than the sun, the most glorious and the brightest of all objects within human knowledge, could express the radiant glories of Jesus' face, when His heavenly nature shone through the veil of His flesh—lightening forth from the inward radiance. And that transfiguration radiance was not the reflection of a great light shining *upon* Him, but the manifestation of such a condition of purity and deity and glory *within* as to be seen breaking through the very flesh and form of His body. The suffusing splendor of that inner light had always been in Jesus incarnate, even as the potentialities of transfiguring glory were ever present to Christ's spirit.

Jesus, during the days of his flesh on earth, was "God's great lamp shining in this dark world, but with the wick of his essential deity turned low, even though the flame of Godhood, though suppressed, flowed there all the while within the white crystal of His enveloping humanity, steadily manifesting a glory"— a "glory as of the only begotten of the Father, full of grace and truth" (John 1:14). "But in that epochal and transcendent hour His person, suddenly charged with the intensified effulgence of deity, burst forth in full flame"—flashing forth in radiancy unrestrained, the temple of His body blazing with the dazzling and awe-inspiring splendors of spiritual incandescence.

On no occasion did such stupendously transcendent illumination come as the transfiguration splendor of the sudden surcharge of the outburst of His deity. All the glory which He had with the Father before the world was, which glory the veil of the flesh completely hid, burst forth in its shining fulness. Here, in this glorious transfiguring hour, the disciples saw Him revealed as perfect manhood and holy God-hood in one glorious Personality. Dr. Freeman says that if there had been the slightest flaw in the life of Jesus He

could not have endured the sudden voltage which sur-
charged Him there on the mountain peak. And he goes
on to show, as we all need to be told, that though a
cracked crystal might stand the lighter test of a low-
burning wick, the cracked crystal cannot bear the shock
of sudden and assaulting heat, for the full-forced flame
would find the flaw and shatter the glass. And then,
with words that almost stun us, he says:

"Had Christ been less than God's perfect man, He
would have died upon the mount. The shock of the
sudden glory would have slain Him. It would have
been to Him a consuming fire. The transfiguration
means that that deity blazing up in Jesus, in instantane-
ous and full effulgence, found His manhood a flawless
crystal. So perfectly had His human life been moulded
to the Father's will that He was able to receive, without
strain, the full flame of Godhood. So purely had He
lived, so completely had He been the truth, that even
the flashing through Him of that light ineffable, before
which the seraphim veil their faces, disclosed in Him
no speck or stain. The experience on the mount marked
the consummation of His personal human perfection.
There and then His perfect manhood burst into brilliant flower. Had He not been in the world for redemp-
tive purposes, God would have plucked the flower then
and laid it in His bosom."

That transfiguration night of solitude and companionship, in which, as never before, they saw Him as perfect
man and holy God by manifestation, was to them a sun
all their lives — and that spiritual incandescence of
His deity caused them ever to know Him as perfect
manhood and holy Godhood.

And now we think of

III — THE TALKING — *"And there talked with him
two men."*

*And, behold, there talked with him two men, which
were Moses and Elias: who appeared in glory, and
spake of his decease which he should accomplish at
Jerusalem.*—LUKE 9: 30-31

There appeared unto the disciples two men — human
beings — Moses and Elijah. They appeared in glory—
in their glorified bodies — something like that of the
transfigured Jesus, but with less radiance. Moses was
the man of Sinai. Elijah was the man of Carmel.
Moses, impressing a world with the loftiness of his
early leadership, was the founder of the nation. Elijah
was the reformer of the nation. Moses gave the nation—
under God — a charter. Elijah — under God — called
the nation back to allegiance. The waters of the Red
Sea divided themselves at the stroke of the rod of Moses.
The waters of the Jordan were divided at the touch
of the folded sheepskin of Elijah. Moses, "around
his single will's unpliant stem," gathered from a host
of wanderers a commonwealth whose law and religion
were one. Elijah was the personal force which "carried
the impulse of the human soul in Israel over an abyss
and, in Elisha, made it pre-eminent in civilizing power."
Both Moses and Elijah had fasted forty days. So had
Jesus fasted forty days. Both of these men were marvelous in their lives, and both were removed from the
earth in a strange manner. Moses had no sooner tasted
of death than he was withdrawn from under the do-
minion of death and of him that had the power of death
(Deut. 34:6 and Jude 9).

Elijah had not died — had never had the death dew
upon his brow — had never had the death ice to stiffen

his fingers. But he was taken up in a chariot of fire, during which flaming flight his natural body was changed into a spiritual body (II Kings 2:11 and I Cor. 15:51).

And thus with their resurrection bodies they were peculiarly fitted to appear on this occasion as examples of the complete redemption of man, for which Jesus came to earth. Both these men on a mountain had seen visions of God. Both pointed to Christ as Savior and testified beforehand of His sufferings and the glory that should follow. They were the two most remarkable characters in the whole of the Mosaic colony. Moses, standing now actually in the Promised Land for the first time, was the one whose presence signified that, in Jesus, "the shadows of the law were all fulfilled and now withdrawn." Elijah's presence testified that in this transfigured Christ, all the hope of heaven begins and ends, and that, in Him, "every prophecy of the past is fulfilled." Moses was the representative of the Law. Through him the law was given, and the kingdom founded, and the sacrifices instituted which prefigured the sacrifice of Christ. Elijah was the representative of the Prophets, who foretold the coming of the Messiah, His sufferings, and His kingly glory, while he was himself the type of the forerunner. Jesus Christ in His own person brought the Gospel, the fulfillment and completion of the other two, "so I shall not remain in the law and the prophets, but through the law and the prophets I shall come to Christ."

And there was a conference of these three. "And they were talking with Jesus." Moses, with the flash of God's throne in his eye and the life of eternity in his voice, talking with Jesus. Elijah, feeling the security of a yearning past in the grandeur of the present, reading in the shining face of Jesus the unwritten harmony

of the song of Moses and that of the Lamb, talking
with Jesus. They "spake of his decease which he was
about to accomplish at Jerusalem" — not concerning the
brilliancy of His transfigured face, or even the rapture
of the blest. The word here translated "decease" is the
Greek word "exodus," similar to our English word
"decease," meaning "a going away." It is used in only
two other places in the New Testament. In Hebrews
11:22 it refers to the exodus of the Israelites from
Egypt, in which, of course, Moses was the great leader.
In II Peter 1:15 the apostle uses it with reference to
his own approaching death.

They were talking, not merely of the crucifixion and
the bloody cross down the road a distance. They were
talking of His exodus, His departure, from this earth
by a threefold way — by the cross, by the resurrection,
and by the ascension. It was not the end of Jesus'
existence, but an episode in His life. For His life on
earth was an episode between two eternities, one reach-
ing back before all worlds, one forward forever.

The Cross — with all its bloody horrors. The resurrection — with all its joy and triumphs and glories.
The ascension, when, with the cloud as His chariot and
the winds as His steeds, He went back to the Father's
right hand. Of these were they talking. They were
not talking of Christ's irreproachable life, not talking
of Christ's matchless teachings, not talking of Christ's
astonishing miracles, not talking of Christ's marvelous
example. Incidental and collateral all these to the one
purpose for which He came — to die, that man born
once and born dead might be born again and born
alive.

Talking, they were, of His exodus — His departure
from this world by the cross, where Jesus became for

us all that God must judge, by the resurrection, the cer-
tificate of our Lord's mission from heaven, and by the
ascension, when "a cloud received him out of their
sight."

That brings us now to think of

IV — TABERNACLES.

*Then answered Peter, and said unto Jesus, Lord, it
is good for us to be here: if thou wilt, let us make
here three tabernacles; one for thee, and one for
Moses, and one for Elias.*—MATT. 17:4

Luke tells us that Peter said this "not knowing what
he said." Peter knew the words he was speaking, but
he did not know the significance thereof.

Now Peter had said and had done some foolish
things in his life. But never *said* he, never *did* he a
more foolish thing, than when he suggested the building of three tabernacles there on the mountain which
he later called "the holy mount." Foolish was Peter
yonder in the coasts of Caesarea Philippi, as Matthew
tells us about it, when he "took him and began to
rebuke him" (Matt. 16: 21-22).

Jesus showed how foolish Peter was when He
said: "Get thee behind me, Satan: thou art an offence
unto me."

Foolish was Peter yonder in the upper room when
Jesus "began to wash the disciples' feet, and to wipe
them with the towel wherewith he was girded" (John
13: 6-9).

Foolish was Peter when Christ's enemies, a great
multitude, came "with lanterns and torches and weapons" to arrest Jesus (John 18: 10-11). And please let
me ask you never to think that Peter meant to cut the
poor man's ear off. Do not ever accuse him of meaning

to do that. He just meant to split his head wide open.
And the only reason he did not was that his aim was bad.

Foolish was Peter the night of the betrayal when he
denied Jesus and "began to curse and swear, saying, I
know not this man of whom you speak" (Mark 14:71).

Foolish was Peter, too, when, concerning John, he
asked of Jesus, "Lord, and what shall this man do?"
(John 21:21).

But Peter never spoke more foolishly, in my judgment, than he did amidst the glory of the transfiguration hour when he suggested the building of three
tabernacles — one for Christ, one for Moses and one
for Elijah. Furnishing us an example of a piety that
has not "been burdened in his death," not yet has "risen
with Christ," he spoke "not knowing what he said."
Peter's talk was trivial twitter and twaddle. Not because what he said was impractical. Not because it
was so natural for Peter to blurt out things thought-
lessly. Not because he desired to stay in such elect
heavenly company. Not because he desired to remain
forever in a sweetly delectable and spiritual gathering.
Not because Peter was acting selfishly. I do not agree
with those who say that Peter indicated a selfish spirit—
that he was still hounded by Christ's saying regarding
the cross and that he felt it would be so much better
to stay on the transfiguration mountain than to be travel-
ing in the valley towards Calvary. Though I do not
walk with the presumptuous step of a know-it-all, I do
not think Peter was thinking so much about how much
better it was to be there on the mount than to descend
into the plain and wrestle with sin, unbelief and disease — so much better than to go back into the world
and resume the wearying conflict.

Selfishness, I believe, was not the sin of Peter and

his thoughtless suggestion on the mountain. But this: In the panic of his soul, he laid hold mentally on Moses and Elijah, those two great men vouchsafed from the unseen, as means of estimating Christ, "instead of clinging to Jesus as the one personal Fact which then and there flooded the whole past with such a radiance that all its steps must seem a divine path." He was foolishly guilty of putting Jesus on a level with the greatest of men — finding no infinite difference between the leader and lawgiver of Israel and God's prophet of fire and Jesus, the Savior of men. And Peter was guilty of what many, dwelling on some Hermon-height of culture are guilty of today — possessing a soul whose spiritual life knows no difference between the touch of the infinite Christ and the influence of the mighty spirits who cleared the way for Him. Peter was guilty of the terrible foolishness and sin of Pharaoh of Egypt, who said to Moses, "Sacrifice in the land" — after God had said, "Go a three days' journey into the wilderness." Just as Pharaoh was guilty of putting the religion of Jehovah on a par with the religion of Egypt — putting God on a level with the gods of Egypt — so Peter was guilty of the terrible sin and foolishness of putting Jesus on a level with the greatest of men. Peter was putting Jesus on a level with the prophets — and no man can do that without appearing as ridiculous as a clown guffawing levity at a funeral.

No man can speak a word that puts Jesus on a level with the greatest that ever lived among men without speaking in sin. No man can preach a sermon that puts Jesus on a level with earth's greatest without preaching a sermon that approaches blasphemy. No man can write a line that puts Jesus on a level with the greatest figures of history without writing sinful words. No man can think a thought that puts Jesus in the same mold with earth's greatest prophets without thinking sin. No man can publish a book that puts Jesus in the same scales of earth's noblest characters without having in that book that which is foul to the holy nostrils of God. Jesus is forever the GREAT UNLIKE. He moved in a moral realm above the intellects and saints of earth and time, thus showing that the law of genius cannot claim Him, for "genius hath its several fixed orbits."

When we mention Jesus, there is no one to stand beside Him. He stands alone, august, unique, supreme. His name is above every name and with Him no mortal can compare among the sons of men. Charles Lamb was right who said: "If all the illustrious men were gathered together and Shakespeare should enter their shining company they would all rise to do him honor. But, if Jesus Christ should come, we would all kneel to *worship Him.*" And Napoleon is right who confesses: "I know men, and I tell you Jesus is not a man. Comparison is impossible between Him and any other being in the world. He is truly a Being by Himself." And Emerson is right who, when asked why he did not include Jesus among his "representative men," confesses the glistening garments which Jesus wears by saying, "It takes too much strength of constitution to do that."

It is only as the Son of God that Christ's wonderful life and character and person in the least can be comprehended. That is why Paul, by the Holy Ghost, wrote:

> *Who, being in the form of God, thought it not robbery to be equal with God: but made himself of no reputation, and took upon him the form of a servant, and was made in the likeness of men: And being found in fashion as a man, he humbled himself, and*

> *became obedient unto death, even the death of the*
> *cross. Wherefore God also hath highly exalted him,*
> *and given him a name which is above every name:*
> *that at the name of Jesus every knee should bow, of*
> *things in heaven, and things in earth, and things*
> *under the earth; and that every tongue should confess*
> *that Jesus Christ is Lord, to the glory of God the*
> *Father.*—PHIL. 2: 6-11

He is highly exalted today. His name absorbs all other
names. Having submitted to the lowest humiliation, He
sits now upon the highest throne.

We consider now

V — THE TESTIMONY — *"A voice out of the cloud*
           which said."

> *While he yet spake, behold, a bright cloud over-*
> *shadowed them: and behold a voice out of the cloud,*
> *which said, This is my beloved Son, in whom I am*
> *well pleased; hear ye him.*—MATT. 17:5

"A bright cloud overshadowed them"— a cloud in
which the visitors departed. It was Shekinah glory
cloud, such as hid Jesus from view when He ascended
up to heaven and such as He will return in to earth
"yet a little while." The cloud symbolized mystery.
The brightness suggested glory. "Behold a voice out
of the cloud," "hear ye him." As though God, with
pity and with interrupting compassion, was saying,
"Shut up, Peter." "A voice out of the cloud which
said, 'This is my beloved Son, in whom I am well
pleased.'" That voice, the voice of God, the same voice
which was heard from the clouds of Sinai and the
clouds at Jesus' baptism, saying, "This is my beloved
Son." The voice of the Father seals the deity of Jesus.
That voice was a testimony to His sinlessness — to
God's approval of all He said and of all He did and

of all He was to say and to do. That voice of heavenly approval testified that Jesus illustrated in His daily life every doctrine of His heavenly mind. While others were calling Jesus a criminal, God was testifying to His sinlessness. While some others were calling Him a bastard, casting slurs upon his virgin birth, God was calling Him "my beloved Son." While some others, in their enmity and hatred of Jesus, were calling Him a liar and a wine-bibber and a glutton and a deceiver, God was saying, "My beloved Son in whom I am well pleased."

As you never find foul odors in flowers, so you find no ruins of bad habits in Christ's character. As fire is always warm, so Christ's moral earnestness is always at white heat. As snow leaves no sooty marks on the earth, so circumstances leave no fingerprints upon His conduct. As no deaf man is ever disturbed by noise, so the most splendid popularity never quickened a pulse beat. As a toy hammer cannot beat the pyramids down, so the most dreadful misfortune does not loosen a fiber. He is always at His best. He is never betrayed into an error of judgment. He never hurried a footstep — because of popularity. He never falters in a purpose — because of antagonism. He was so finely strung, so unutterably keyed to truth and to mercy and to justice and to love and so quickly felt the sorrow, the sympathy and the indignation which wrong and injustice invariably elicit from all high souls.

Though history bears witness that governments oft ignore Him, still He is well pleasing to God. Though self-exploiting demagogues, swayed by ulterior motives, find nothing desirable for them in His ministry, still He is ever well pleasing to God. Though the money changers, expert in illicit traffic, despised Him, still God is well pleased with Him. Though knotty lawyers, skillful in turning the law against the innocent, hated Him, God spake, saying, "I am well pleased." Though the scribes, buried in precedents and legalism, hated Him, still God spake, saying, "I am well pleased with him." Though the materialistic Sadducees, denying a divine hope to the travail of the ages, also hated Him, God was ever well pleased with Him. Though the Greek, with his wild mythologies pitied Him, God was well pleased with Him. Though the Roman with his gross materialism considered what He said and did as the wild nightmare of a disordered brain, still God was well pleased with Him. Though the priests, with their self-righteous creeds, abhorred Him, still was God well pleased with Him. Though the stately rabbis, looking at Him out of envious eyes, considered Him a fly in their ointment, still God was well pleased with Him. Though the kings of His day slighted Him and the rich sometimes flouted Him, still, in it all, God was well pleased with Him. Even though His friends, on certain occasions, thought Him beside Himself (Mark 3:21), still God is well pleased with Him who has bannered continents with love and changed the climate of nations.

VI — THE TOUCH — *"And Jesus came and touched them."*

> *And when the disciples heard it, they fell on their face, and were sore afraid. And Jesus came and touched them, and said, Arise, and be not afraid.*
> —MATT. 17: 6-7

Thus He met their emergency — with calmness and comfort. With tranquility He met the emergencies of the poor, the obscure, the publican, the outcast, the sinner, the king, the scholar, the slave. He touched them and spoke. What a touch it was! What a voice they

heard! Hillis said: "Christ had a mighty touch. He
touched poetry and clothed it with power. He touched
marriage and turned it into romance and love. And
Christ is ready now to touch work and wages and turn
them into sacraments of human fellowship." With that
thought in mind, I want you to think upon the touch of
Christ. He touched the slave —and his shackles fell off.
He touched the weak — and they became too strong to
be oppressed. He touched the home — and it became a
house of delight. He touched the cradle — and the
childhood became sacred. He touched music — and it
became pure and sweet. He touched art — and the
canvas took on lustrous beauty. He touched architec-
ture — and it became worthy of man's worship of God.

His touch took away fear. "Arise, be not afraid."
That touch, comforting them, gave them courage.
We touch people every day. Sometimes a physical
touch — a hand laid on their shoulder, hand held for
a moment in theirs, flash of eye as we pass on street,
casual conversation with unknown people in a shop or
on train or street car or garage or church. What do
we leave behind us? What is the quality of our contact
with people? What is the essence of personality we
communicate? Is our touch defiling, degrading, de-
pressing, chilly? Does our touch awaken hatred and
distrust? Does our touch bring folks into a spiritual
world?

Jesus touched eyes — and they saw. Jesus touched
ears — and they heard. Jesus touched hands — and
they worked. Jesus touched hearts — and they rejoiced.
Jesus touched feet — and they served. Jesus touched
mouths — and they spoke. May our eyes, our ears, our
hands, our feet, our mouths be touched!

God touched my eyes, from out the mists
I saw a flaming Paradise.

God touched my ears. I heard their cry
As hunger-riven souls passed by.

God touched my feet and they became
Wings—brilliant, beautiful and fleet.

God touched my knees. In prayer
They bent for those all crushed with care.

God touched my tongue, and I did seek
His messages of truth and love to speak.

God touched my heart. All men became
Those I must love—all in His name.

And now, as we depart from this continent of truth,
let us consider

VII — The Torments — *"My son . . . he is lunatick
and sore vexed."*

*And when they were come to the multitude, there
came to him a certain man, kneeling down to him,
and saying, Lord, have mercy on my son: for he is
lunatick, and sore vexed: for ofttimes he falleth into
the fire, and oft into the water. And I brought him
to thy disciples, and they could not cure him. Then
Jesus answered and said, O faithless and perverse
generation, how long shall I be with you? how long
shall I suffer you? Bring him hither to me. And
Jesus rebuked the devil; and he departed out of him:
and the child was cured from that very hour.*—MATT.
17:14-18

"And when they were come to the multitude." While
the communion of saints in heavenly places is uplifting,
the disciples of the Lord have their duties in the valleys. One cannot stay in the mountain continually. In
fact, one goes up into the mountain only that he may
be better prepared for the work on the plain. Those

who permanently remain in the mount of religious exaltation are not of great benefit to broken, impoverished,
lost humanity.

They came down from the mountain — from the top
to the tormented. They were not to live "in that high
mountain apart," or pine in solitary places. But they
could take the mountain down into the valley where
the lunatic was tormented and where the father was
tormented in heart and soul because of his tormented
boy — and where many others were tormented with
heartaches and burdens and soul agonies and needed
prompting in their perplexities, help in their hazards,
direction in their doubts, guidance in their glooms, comfort in their sorrows. If people can go to the mountain
lands and cross mountain heights and come back without bringing the mountains with them, they have gone
there and have been there in vain. But when people
can bring the mountain with its cooling snows and
spiritual experiences back with them, the mountain
will be the root and source of sustenance during the
whole period of suffering and divers ministries. Does
an orchestra ever meet for rehearsal for the purpose
of hanging their instruments on the wall? No, but for
the building of rhythmic palaces of melody before the
eyes of the souls of people that they may be blessed,
and strengthened. How long will it take us to learn
that God grants us white and shining revelations of
Himself and of His purpose that we may go down the
mountain and heal the lunatic that is raving at its base—
a misery to himself, a wretchedness and joy-quencher
to others? We cannot look spiritually from Hermon
without looking by the way of the cross, and, through
its crimson lenses, seeing the multitudes "in the valley."

Let us learn that tabernacles at the top when there

are forgotten torments in the valley are so incongruous.
Let us know assuredly that sweet singing at the top
without concern for those in sorrow in the valley loses its
sweetest melodies. Let us remember ever that soulful
sayings *about* Him on the mountain top without scar
service *for* Him in the valley is so unlike what He asks
of us. Let us forget never that worship in the mountain
that is not followed by work in the valley is a strange
worship. Let us "punch ourselves through" with the
conviction that tabernacles at the top unrelated to the
taint and trials and temptations in the valley are but
rebellions against God's good will.

After our mountain meetings and high festivals of
rapture and our supreme hours of joy, let us go down
the mountain to re-affirm and to heal. You cannot approach a multitude without finding afflictions. Jesus did
not come down to talk about the top. He came down to
the folks — to heal their lunacy, to soothe their pain, to
comfort their unutterable distresses. Surely the mountain top experiences of the disciples at the Transfiguration and the multitudes in the valley were not far from
the thought kingdom of one who wrote and prayed:

> Lord, let me not stay at the top of the ladder
> though the top be heaven.
> Send me down to days of danger,
> Send me down to nights of sorrow,
> Send me down to souls that are sad,
> Send me down to places where the shadows are,
> Send me down to people bound with burdens,
> Send me down with a breath of Paradise,
> Send me down with a flower from Eden,
> Send me down with a cluster of the grapes of
> Canaan.

Send me down to hearts that are homeless, to homes
that are heartless, to lives that are loveless, to loves that

are lifeless, to crowds without a compass, to ranks without a refuge, to prodigals at the hog trough, to churches that are drifting sepulchres manned by frozen crews, to multitudes unled and misled. Send me down to be a blessing. Send me down from the top to the torment. Send me down from the peaks to the perishing. Send me down from the summits to the sinning. Send me down from the spiritual peaks to a participation in the affairs of men, helping them to bear life's burdens with greater strength and to face life's perilous situations with braver hearts. And then and there and everywhere we shall experience for ourselves the truth of what Mrs. Browning believed, who wrote:

> A child's kiss set on thy sighing lips
> Shall make thee glad.
> A poor man helped by thee
> Shall make thee rich.
> A sick one nursed by thee
> Shall give thee health.
> A sad one comforted by thee
> Shall bring thee joy.
> Thy love shall shout its own beatitudes
> After its own life workings.

Moreover, we shall bring to others the blessings of our own obedience to the words of Jesus, who said:

Let your light so shine before men, that they may see your good works, and glorify your Father which is in heaven.—MATT. 5:16

CHAPTER TWO

S I N

Wherefore, as by one man sin entered into the world, and death by sin; and so death passed upon all men, for that all have sinned.—ROMANS 5:12

Moreover the law entered, that the offence might abound. But where sin abounded, grace did much more abound.—ROMANS 5:20

I — MY PURPOSE

In this sermon I hope that I shall give no impression that I walk with the presumptuous step of a know-it-all. I hope to give no little answers to big questions. I want to suggest truths to be meditated on in quiet hours, to furnish food for those who hunger after righteousness, to provide shield and sword and spear against the enemies of men's souls, to warn men to flee from the wrath to come, to point the way and open the gates to the city of refuge for sinners. I have no desire to be a photographer of sordid spots or a careless prober of abscesses. And certainly I do not lift my voice in the belief that I shall be able to reclaim all who have gone astray. But I speak with the hope and prayer that I shall warn all who need the warning of God's Word, causing them to see that sin is a destroying and

31

killing thing, helping them to know that death and destruction come in by sin's door, enabling them to
believe that if they do not well "sin croucheth at the
door." For, as Jowett says, the sorest injury we can do
to any man is to lighten his conception of the enormity
of sin. Surely then, only fools make a mock of sin.
One of the glories of evangelical religion is that it
never makes light of sin. It would have us remember
that:

> Sin is a monster of such frightful mien
> Which to be hated needs but to be seen;
> But seen too oft, familiar with its face,
> We first endure, then pity, then embrace.

One purpose, among other purposes, is to help you
get a vision of God's holiness and see the horrors of
sin; for never do I covet a phraseology that lends re-
spectability to sin, and forever do I hate all euphemisms
that would call sin's poison only a slightly pernicious
peppermint. Nothing in all the universe is more destruc-
tive of all happiness than sin. Sin has ruined angels
and men. Sin, the most terrible fact in human history,
has caused every tear of sorrow, every sigh of grief,
every pang of agony. Sin, as a stoker that feeds the
hot fires of passion, has withered everything that is fair.
Sin, blackening human history from Eden to the present
day, has blasted everything that is good, and made bitter
everything that is sweet. Sin, its habitat everywhere,
has dried up every spring of comfort. Sin, with a
geography which cannot be changed, has rolled a tide
of sorrow far and wide.

Sin, as a corrupting corrosion, strikes its roots deep
into the center of the soul, generating therein a worm
which shall never die, kindling therein a fire never to
be quenched. Sin, a loathsome disease, spreads death

over the whole moral man. Sin, terrible as a tornado,
darkens the understanding and hardens the heart. Sin,
oft silent as poison, sears the conscience and makes
rebellious the will. Sin, the weaver of all shrouds and
the maker of all the coffins of men and the digger of
all of earth's graves, offers to sick humanity the greatest
imposture of a medicine that was ever placed on the
market. Sin, a direct contrariety to the holiness of
God, is the flashiest concern that ever lured an unsus-
pecting public. Yet what multitudes take sin's prospec-
tus as if it were gilt-edged security! But every man
starts on the road to spiritual and moral bankruptcy
when he invests his capital in sin, for sin pays only in
counterfeit coin, offers the honey that is all gall, leads
the thirsty only to broken cisterns that hold no water.
Surely Ralph Barton, noted journalist and caricaturist,
dying by his own hand in his New York apartment,
had found that out, when despair came as when
"through the torn sail the wild tempest is streaming"—
and he wrote:

> I have had my will,
> Tasted every pleasure;
> I have drunk my fill
> Of the purple measure.
> It has lost its zest;
> Sorrow is my guest;
> Oh, the lees are bitter, bitter—
> Give me rest.
>
> Love once filled my bowl,
> Running over with blisses;
> Made my very soul
> Drunk with crimson kisses.
> But I drank it dry;
> Love has passed me by.
> Oh, the lees are bitter, bitter—
> Let me die.

May such words help many to see that sin is, no matter what disguise it uses, the death head set amidst
life's feast — help many, who fain would pamper their
flesh to the destruction of their souls, know that sin's
breath, no matter how perfumed and concoctionally
scented, is the desert breath that drinks up every dew.

II — OUR FIRST PARENTS

1. Man was made in the image of God. No fact is
more clearly set forth in the Bible than the fact that
man came into this world by the direct creative act of
God. Man, created in holiness, created for the glory
of God, was not "evolved by nature."

> *So God created man in his own image, in the image of
> God created he him; male and female created he
> them.*—GENESIS 1:27

> *And God saw everything that he had made, and, be-
> hold, it was very good.*—GENESIS 1:31

> *Lo, this only have I found, that God hath made man
> upright; but they have sought out many inventions.*
> —ECCLES. 7:29

It is distinctly uplifting thus to learn the truth.
Rational as the fact of God, inspiring as the truth that
there is a Designer behind all design, in beautiful agree-
ment with Christian experience is the story of creation
just as it stands in the first and second chapters of
Genesis.

> *And God said, Let us make man in our image, after
> our likeness: and let them have dominion over the
> fish of the sea, and over the fowl of the air, and
> over the cattle, and over all the earth, and over every
> creeping thing that creepeth upon the earth.*
> —GENESIS 1:26

Thus, after the triune God counseled together concerning the act about to be performed, there was the

execution of this determined purpose of God — to cre-
ate the human soul and to frame for it a body for its
dwelling place and organ — the mind and the body
compatible and complementary. Thus man, allied to
heaven, related to God Himself, came into glorious
being. "Image," we are told, denotes likeness in out-
ward form, while the substance may be different. "Likeness," a more general term, indicates resemblance in
any quality, external or internal.

God is a Spirit.

> *God is a Spirit: and they that worship him must*
> *worship him in spirit and in truth.*—JOHN 4:24

As a spirit He thinks, speaks, wills, acts. And reason,
speech, will, and power are the great points of con-
formity to God in man. In the reason is enthroned the
distinction of good and evil. In the will is unfolded
that freedom of action which chooses the good and
refuses the evil. Murphy says: "In the spiritual being
that exercises reason and will resides the power to act,
which pre-supposes both these faculties, the reason as
informing the will, and the will as directing the power."

Now God is invisible.

> *No man hath seen God at any time; the only begotten*
> *Son, which is in the bosom of the Father, he hath*
> *declared him.*—JOHN 1:18

And Jesus is called "the *image* of the *invisible* God"
(Col. 1:15). Since God is spirit and, as spirit, is invisible, He has no material form. Therefore, the
"image" and the "likeness" is not physical, but moral
and spiritual. It is described as righteousness and true
holiness. Paul, in Ephesians 4:4, says: "Put on the
new man which after God is *created* in righteousness
and true holiness." And in Col. 3:10, we read: "And

have put on the new man which is renewed in knowledge
after the *image* of him that created him." As God was
holy, the very embodiment of perfection, so man was
created holy. Nor was this holiness merely an accident
or a super-added quality, but was inherent in the very
nature and constitution of our first parents.

But sin wounded and slew our first parents in paradise, which is to say that—

III — MAN, BY VOLUNTARY TRANSGRESSION, FELL, AND THEN SIN ENTERED THE WORLD

*Wherefore, as by one man sin entered into the world,
and death by sin; and so death passed upon all men,
for that all have sinned.*—ROMANS 5:12

While man was created perfect, he was created a
man, and not a *machine*. He was endowed with the
power of choice. So endowed, he could choose obedience or disobedience. He, with a body divinely fashioned in Eden, a body not out of harmony with the
divine form and essence, and with a mental nature of
the same kind of essence as the being of God, made
the wrong choice. And this wrong choice was made
voluntarily — prompted by the enticing influence of
Satan — Satan, who "fumbles with the fool and capers
with culture, who sighs with the sad and frolics with
the frivolous, who prays with the pious and vies with
the vicious, who plods with the poor and races with
the rich, who pines with the peasant and romps with
the royalty," who ambles in the aisles and by the altars
of sanctuaries and lounges in the lazaretto, who sings
with the saint and sneers with the cynic. So, Satan, an
evil cosmopolite, so at home in every place and in any
society, so persistently about his diabolical work, with
his wiles and devices and ministers and wrath and

power, seeking whom he may devour, wrought havoc in
Eden. Thus man voluntarily departed from God — and
ceased to be the innocent being which God had made.
God, by a direct creative act, made man. But He did not
make a *sinful* man. God made man. That man made
a *choice*. That choice was *sin*. Adam, the first man,
was not deceived.

> *And Adam was not deceived, but the woman being
> deceived was in the transgression.*—I Timothy 2:14

He acted voluntarily — deliberately — and was, therefore, a voluntary transgressor.

So sin destroyed our first parents. It destroyed them
as to the peace of their conscience, for it made them
hide themselves.

> *And they heard the voice of the Lord God walking
> in the garden in the cool of the day: and Adam and
> his wife hid themselves from the presence of the Lord
> God amongst the trees of the garden.*—Genesis 3:8

It destroyed them as to the state of their souls, for it
made them both legally dead, under the law sentence,
and so liable to eternal death — and it made them
spiritually dead under the power of sin, according to
that threatening.

> *And you hath he quickened, who were dead in tres-
> passes and sins.*—Ephesians 2:1

> *And unto Adam he said, Because thou hast harkened
> unto the voice of thy wife, and hast eaten of the tree,
> of which I commanded thee, saying, Thou shalt not
> eat of it: cursed is the ground for thy sake; in sorrow
> shalt thou eat of it all the days of thy life.*
> —Genesis 2:17

It destroyed them as to the life of their body, for
quickly the body became mortal, subject to all out-

ward miseries, which are a *temporal* death, and to the
dissolution of soul and body, which is *natural* death.

Now Adam's sin did not affect him alone. As by
him *sin* entered this world and *death* by sin, "so death
passed upon all men, for that *all* have sinned." All
men, by conception and birth, are in sin — all hell-
bound and hell-deserving. Adam by his fall received
a corrupt nature. In this condition, he begat sons in
his own sinful image — and thus that corrupt nature
was transmitted to his descendants.

But the question comes — from some: "But how is
man to be held responsible for Adam's sin when he had
nothing to do with that sin which he committed? How
are we to be held responsible for Adam's sin?" Dr.
Len Broughton who, for so many years, walked mightily
among us, wisely answers that question. He says: "The
question grows out of the failure to recognize the
federal headship of Adam. Adam is the federal head
of the race of mankind, and as such he gives coloring
to all his children. And for Adam's sin the world is
suffering. It cannot be otherwise. I remember when I
was in England during the Boer War, I found that very
few of the people were in favor of that war, but the
federal head of that government declared war, and to
war they had to go." Continuing that thought, I say that
so it was also with my mother's father who had never believed in secession, who believed less in slavery. He did
not have any slaves on his farm to defend. He did not
care to defend the slaves of other men. He loved the
furrows of the field far more than the fury of the blood-
wet promiscuous ditches of war. He loved the flame on
the old hearthstone more than the flames of campfires.
He loved the voice of the mockingbird more than the
moan of war drums. He loved the bleating of the flocks

more than the thunder of cannon. Though brave as the bravest, he said war was folly and that every question settled by war could be settled better some other way. He wanted no part ever in war's crimson terrors. Yet he had to go to war just the same. And he lost an arm in battle. But the federal head said "war"— and to war he went. Adam plunged into sin, and all the race of mankind plunged with him — because he was the federal head of the race.

"Trees and plants beget their kind — in appearance, nature, and qualities! Man begets his kind, like begetting like. Therefore, we are often told in Scripture of the obliquities of character descending from the parents to the children, through several generations. Our first parents sinned, and their sin diseased their constitutions — and, according to the laws of cause and effect, like begetting like, their diseased constitutions descended to their children. Their disease was constitutional, and only constitutional diseases are hereditary; being constitutional, they are always hereditary; therefore, their constitutional disease affected without exception all their descendants."

Considering the nature of Adam's transgression and the circumstances under which it was committed, we will see that it was a sin, a crime, of the greatest enormity. It was gross infidelity — in believing the devil rather than God. It was discontent and envy — thinking God had denied him what was essential to his happiness. It was prodigious pride — in desiring to be like God. It was sacrilegious theft — in purloining what God had reserved to Himself as a token of His sovereignty. It was suicide and murder — in bringing sin and death upon him and all posterity.

Just here we should note a most dangerous and insidious and ruinous doctrine taught in the world today. It is: "We are by nature children of God." Paul says:

> *Among whom also we all had our conversation in times past in the lusts of our flesh, fulfilling the desires of the flesh and of the mind; and were by nature the children of wrath, even as others.*—EPHESIANS 2:3

We are *not* by nature children of God. But by grace through faith we become children of God.

> *For ye are all the children of God by faith in Christ Jesus.*—GALATIANS 3:26

> *But as many as received him, to them gave he power to become the sons of God, even to them that believe on his name.*—JOHN 1:12

We are sinners by birth and aliens by practice. "Created by a holy God for holy ends, man sins with his body, heart, mind, head, face, eyes, ears, lips, tongue, palate, stomach, arms, hands, feet." We are totally depraved. And please do not reject this doctrine of total depravity — as the manner of some is. The rejection of the doctrine of total depravity is usually due to a misconception of the doctrine. Total depravity does not mean that one is as mean as Satan nor that he is corrupt as he might be. It means that when man fell the *whole* man fell, and *all* men fell. It means that no part of man escaped the fall, nor any number of men escaped the fall. The great Paul did not say that in Adam *some* fell, but that *all* fell. Nor did he say that in Adam all *partly* fell, but that in Adam all *fell*. Sin wrought havoc with the *race* — not *part* of the race.

> *And God saw that the wickedness of man was great in the earth, and that every imagination of the thoughts of his heart was only evil continually.*
> —GENESIS 6:5

But, let us ask,

IV — WHAT IS SIN ?

Here definition falls short of expressing all that sin is and all that sin does even as a teacup lacks capacity to hold an ocean, even as a spoon lacks strength to tunnel a mountain. But sin is a coming short of the glory — the holy perfection — of God, the object of man's creation.

> *For all have sinned, and come short of the glory of God.*—ROMANS 3:23

> *Even every one that is called by my name: for I have created him for my glory, I have formed him; yea, I have made him.*—ISAIAH 43:7

Sin is "transgression of the law" (I John 3:4). "All unrighteousness is sin" (I John 5:17). "Knowing to do good and doing it not" (James 4:17). "The thought of foolishness" (Proverbs 24:9). "The imaginations of the thoughts of the unregenerate heart" (Genesis 8:21). "Whatever is not of faith" (Romans 14:23). "A haughty look, a proud heart, the plowing of the wicked" (Proverbs 21:4). "Respect of persons" (James 2:9). "Rejecting Jesus" (John 16:9). "Rebellion and stubbornness" (I Samuel 15:23). "Disobedience" (Jeremiah 3:25). "Backsliding" (Jeremiah 14:7). "Speaking against God" (Leviticus 24:15). "Despising one's neighbor" (Proverbs 14:21). These fifteen statements taken together, their content compiled into one sentence, if vocabularily possible, would be a good *definition*, but not a full *description* of sin.

Somebody said: "If you combine in one the infidelity of Ingersoll, the vileness of Nero, the superman of Nietzsche the monstrous wickedness of Karl Marx' philosophy, the lust of Cleopatra, the worldly ambition of

Pilate, the despising of God by Stalin, the vaulting
military genius of Napoleon, the cruelty of Jezebel,
the murderous intent of Henry VIII, the hatred of
Hitler for the Jews, the traitordom of Judas, you will
have some sort of definition of the Antichrist." Accordingly, put all those fifteen statements just made into
one statement, and you will have a definition of sin not
void of wisdom at all.

Let us consider

V — SOME DESCRIPTIVE STATEMENTS ABOUT SIN

Sin is the tragedy of our universe. Sin, like disease,
is debilitating, deadening, deforming, dooming. Sin is
a God-resisting disposition, because of which man "in
self-deficiency and pride opposes himself to God, and
thereby withdraws himself from the active ministry of
God's life and love." And that God-resisting disposition is anarchy. Sin, a breach in the moral order and
harmony of the universe, works disintegration and con-
fusion. Every step in sin is a step backwards and down-
wards. Sin, a conspiracy against the sovereignty of
God, is a contradiction of His nature, an insult to His
holiness. There is no term, expressive of reproach, expressive of shame, expressive of misery, that the Bible
does not use to express the terror of sin. There is no
image that can produce aversion or fear that is not em-
ployed by the Scriptures to represent sin.

Sin is disobedience, rebellion, treason, murder — the
work of Satan. Sin is ignorance, folly, madness. Sin
is blindness, deafness, dumbness, sickness. Sin is poison,
slavery, plague. Sin is death. Sin built hell. Sin produced the "worm that never dies." Sin kindled "the
fire that shall never be quenched." Sin made "the outer
darkness" where no ray of light ever enters. As it is

said of Nabel, "as the name is, so is the man"; the
same may be observed of sin: as the name is, so is the
thing. Sin is not libeled by any of these dreadful
representations. They are all given us by One who perfectly understands sin, and they fall infinitely short of
the subject. For if we compare sin with other evils, it
will be found substantially to contain them all, and to
be the cause of all. This is the fountain which has em-
bittered all our streams, and the seed which has so
thickly sown the world with wretchedness.

Sin destroys and abuses everything. Sin, a fatal
mischief of the heart, a seed big with future pain and
grief, the quintessence of all horrors, the causative ele-
ment of all world suffering, is no whirlwind creating a
a slight disturbance, but a hot sirocco blasting all
gardens.

No light discord — a thunderbolt that shatters the
organ into splinters, leaving it without shape or tone.

No penknife — a guillotine.

No slight jerk of the hiccoughs — the agonies of
sciatica.

No lame Mephibosheth — a diabolical Jezebel.

No crude catapult — a bursting bomb.

No quiet pool — a maelstrom.

No cool rill — a perpetual lava rush scorching its
way through green fields.

Sin is a viper that fastens its fangs in your soul. Sin
is a whirlpool where the soul is swept away. Sin is a
loathsome disease. Sin is the sexton that digs the grave
in which the soul it put. Sin is a stoker that feeds the
hot fires of passion. Sin is a siren which lures men
with her embrace, and drags them into the surging sea
of ruin. Sin is a storm at sea — snuffing out human
life relentlessly. Sin is a volcano at night — pouring

hot lava on human lives. Sin is a flood in the river of life. Sin is an earthquake, tearing away foundations, etc. Sin is quicksand, sucking the soul down, down, down. Sin is an avalanche.

It is good for us to remember that there is a

VI — Distinction Between Sin and Sins

There is sometimes a little hair-splitting that goes on here. But the distinction is often made between SIN and SINS.

> *If we say that we have no sin, we deceive ourselves, and the truth is not in us.*—I JOHN 1:8

Hamilton: "Sin breaking out into sins, is the mark of the sinful and fallen nature of man." Sins are the visible results which come from sin. But "if we confess our SINS, he is faithful and just to forgive us our sins, and to cleanse us from all unrighteousness" (I John 1:9). "Sin is a *state* and refers to the depraved nature received from Adam." He plunged into sin, and all the race of mankind plunged with him, because he was the *federal head* of the race. What is the consequence of Adam's sin to the world? The consequence is universal *sin* — sin everywhere, among all people, for all time to come. The second consequence is universal death. This sort of universalism I know is true.

But as to the distinction between sin and sins, we speak now. Sins are *acts*, the result or the fruit, of the sinful nature — just as evil things men do come from an evil heart.

> *For from within, out of the heart of men, proceed evil thoughts, adulteries, fornications, murders, thefts, covetousness, wickedness, deceit, lasciviousness, an*

evil eye, blasphemy, pride, foolishness: all these evil
things come from within, and defile the man.
—MARK 7: 21-23

And sin is generic, but sins are specific. *Sin* is character, but *sins* are in conduct. Sin is the center, but sins are the circumference. Sin is the root, but sins are the fruit. Sin is the fountain, but sins are its flow. These wise words of another and the truth thereof we can put before you in another way.

Listen! *Sin* is the tree; *sins* are the fruit of the evil tree. *Sin* is the unstrung lute; *sins* are the jangling inharmonies produced therefrom. *Sin* is the evil lungs; *sins* are the polluted and poisonous breathings that come from every gasp of the lungs. *Sin* is the contaminated reservoir; *sins* are the streams that flow therefrom, carrying pollution and disease as they go. *Sin* is source; *sins* are the secretion. *Sin* is the smouldering volcano; *sins* are the burning sulphurs and blighting lavas and deadly gases that are born within its boiling womb. *Sin* is the hive; *sins* are the deadly hornets that issue therefrom. *Sin* is the sire; *sins* are the sons. *Sin* is the old nature; *sins* are the manifestations of the old nature. *Sin* is what we are, *sins* are what we have done. *Sin* is the fact; *sins* are the act. And our justification is a justification from the facts of sin. "God's glory is His perfection, and everything short of perfection is sin." Lying, stealing, drunkenness, profanity, deception, murder, pride, contention, rebellion, self-righteousness, are pictures which show that we are fallen and sinful.

Consider now—

VII — God's Attitude Toward Sin and Sins and Sinning

It is an attitude of wrath.

For the wrath of God is revealed from heaven against all ungodliness and unrighteousness of men, who hold the truth in unrighteousness.—Romans 1:18

God is *love* when it comes to His attitude toward man. But God is wrath when it comes to His attitude toward sin. The whole fight of God from the time Adam left Eden to the time Christ hung on the cross was against sin. God looks on sin and sinning as you would look on a dagger that pierced your mother's heart as it was thrust therein by the hand of a murderer — with righteous revulsion. God looks on sin as you would look on a rattlesnake if you found it coiled in your baby's bed — with holy hate. God looks on sin as you would look on the vulture that would pick out the eyes of your darling child and leave it blind the rest of its days. God looks on sin as you would look on a buzzard in your dining-room. God looks on sin as you would look on the finger prints of the lust demon on the lily-white throat of your fair daughter. God looks on sin as you would look on the footprint of your home's despoiler. God hates sin. The Bethlehem manger says so. The thorns on His brow and the nails in His hands and the spear in His side and the blood on cheek and chin and knee, blood in drops, blood in rills, blood in pools at the foot of the Cross — all these say so! The Cross says so. The empty tomb in the garden says so.

That must be the greatest evil which is most opposite to the greatest good. In forming our estimate of sin, we are not to judge of it so much by the relation it bears to us, or to our fellow creatures, as by its relation

to God; for against Him it is committed! And every
sin strikes at God as much as if no other being was
affected by it. Notwithstanding its fatal effects with
regard to mankind, we may say to God, of every transgression, "Against thee, thee only, have I sinned and
done this evil in thy sight." Sin is enmity against God,
against His attributes, against His government. God
never yet revealed a design which sin hath not with-
stood. God never yet gave a command which sin has not
trampled underfoot. Sin deposes God from His sovereignty. Sin abuses His goodness. Sin abhors His holiness. Sin vilifies His wisdom. Sin insults and denies
His omniscience, His justice and His power. And hence
nothing is so offensive to God as sin. It is called the
"abominable thing which He hates."

We now ask

VIII — What Should Be Our Attitude Toward Sin?
This our attitude should ever be.

> *Likewise reckon ye also yourselves to be dead indeed
> unto sin, but alive unto God through Jesus Christ our
> Lord.*—Romans 6:11

Somebody asks: "What is the difference between a
saint and a sinner?" And the answer is that the difference is the difference of the grave. "Between the
saint and the sinner is the open grave, and the sinner
is on this side, facing it, and the saint is on the resurrection side, leaving it behind, having conquered it."
He is dead with Christ; he is buried with Christ; he is
risen with Christ! We see from this eleventh verse that
we are to reckon ourselves as dead with Christ — as
buried with Christ — as knowing resurrection with
Christ. "Reckon ye yourselves as dead unto sin."
"Reckon ye yourselves alive unto God through Jesus

Christ our Lord." "Yield yourselves unto God as those
who are alive from the dead." That is to say that we are,
by faith, to accept Christ in His atoning work on the
Cross as our salvation — that we are to treat sin as if
we were dead, and give it no more control over us than
if we were dead. Dead feet do not walk in paths of
sin — no more should our feet. Dead hands do not
work the works of sin — no more should our hands.
Dead ears do not listen to the tempter's voice — no
more should our ears. Dead eyes do not possess "lust
of the eyes"— no more should our eyes. Dead lips do
not have adder's poison under them — no more should
our lips. Dead tongues do not speak wickedness and
falsehood — no more should our tongues. Dead shoulders do not carry the devil's corn to mill — no more
should our shoulders. Dead knees do not bow at Satan's
shrine — no more should our knees. Dead hearts do not
beat in sin — no more should our hearts. Dead bodies
do not yield themselves to impurity — no more should
our bodies.

> *Let not sin therefore reign in your mortal body, that*
> *ye should obey it in the lusts thereof. Neither yield*
> *ye your members as instruments of unrighteousness*
> *unto sin: but yield yourselves unto God, as those that*
> *are alive from the dead, and your members as instru-*
> *ments of righteousness unto God.*—ROMANS 6: 12-13

How glorious our lives, if, reckoning ourselves dead
unto sin but alive unto God, we are "always bearing
about in the body the dying of the Lord Jesus, that the
life also of Jesus might be made manifest in our body."

"Reckon ye yourselves dead!" There were two men,
both preachers; and they were great friends. They went
through the university together, and were both insepar-
able. However, when they graduated, they separated.

One went as a missionary to a far country and the other stayed in England. Before they separated each signed a covenant to this effect: "If you die first, I will preach your funeral sermon; if I die first, you will preach mine." They separated. Years and years passed, and after a while, in the Providence of God, these two ministers met again — and it was a joyful good time when they met. They talked about the various things that had transpired. One finally said to the other, "Look here, do you remember that contract we made when we separated?" "Yes, I do." "Well, you remember that we agreed to write our funeral sermons and keep them until the time of delivery. Did you write yours?" "Yes —did you write yours?" "Have you got your funeral sermon on me?" "Yes; have you got yours on me?" "Well, I declare, isn't that funny? I tell you — you get yours and I will get mine, and let's get together and we will read what we said then just fresh from the University — and we will see if we have changed our opinions."

And so they got together with their sermons. Number One got up to preach the funeral sermon of Number Two. He stood in front of him and began. His oration was very beautiful and his language was perfect. As he piled it on and on and on, Number Two smiled and said: "Hold on!" "No!" said Number One, "you quit that smiling and keep your seat. You are dead; dead people don't talk."

Now that is just exactly what the Apostle means. We are to reckon ourselves dead. We are to act with relation to sin as if we were dead; and sin is to have no more charm, no more influence, and no more lure over our lives than if we were dead. To this uniquely apt incident and to all these words from Dr. Broughton, whom, in my boyhood days I greatly loved and whose memory I now cherish, do we give the best approval of our hearts. God help us as to sin to say: "Not one leaf from its voluptuous petals; not one drop from its cup of abomination; not one spark from its fire of evil; not one step down the stair of its darkness; not one thread from the garment of its pollution; not one touch from the body of shame; not one hour of sleep in its couch of defilement."

If you open your dictionary you will find in the first page that three-fourths of the words owe their existence and significance to sin. Yet it is a fading word in the vocabulary of many. Nothing is more necessary than the recovery of our lost indignation against sin. We need again the old Puritan attitude of fear and shame and torment at the thought of it. We need the conviction that "sin is an offense against God, causing Him infinite pain and arousing His just and awful indignation." How hellish and blasphemous is this statement:

> Have you sinned? It is only an error,
>   Your spirit is pure and white.
> It is Truth's own ray and will find its way
>   Back into the path of right.

Cardinal Newman said: "It is the one great security against sin to be shocked at it." When people say of sin that it is not so bad after all, they use not the grammar of salvation but the grammar of damnation. Call poison by any name you like. Flatter it, camouflage it, if you will. But poison kills just the same. How we all need humbly to pray:

> *For thy name's sake, O Lord, pardon mine iniquity; for it is great.*—PSALM 25:11

We should joyfully now think of

IX — Abounding Grace

> *Moreover the law entered, that the offense might abound. But where sin abounded, grace did much more abound.*—Romans 5:20

Grace is the unlimited and unmerited favor of God to the utterly undeserving — unmerited divine blessing. Grace is God's bestowment upon us the very opposite of all we deserve. Grace fails not when and where we need salvation most.

> As we all by foreign guilt
>   In Adam are reviled;
> Therefore we all by sovereign grace,
>   In Christ are reconciled!

This grace — saving, sealing, sanctifying —is like the Well of Loch Maree in Whittier's song, over which cool shadows lie, and round which are smooth white stones:

> And whoso bathes therein his brow,
>   With care or madness burning,
> Feels once again his healthful thought
>   And sense of peace returning.
>
> O restless heart and fevered brain,
>   Unquiet and unstable,
> That holy well of Loch Maree;
>   Is more than idle fable!
>
> Life's changes vex, its discords stun,
>   Its glaring sunshine blindeth,
> But blest is he who on his way
>   That fount of Healing findeth!
>
> The shadows of a humbled will
>   And contrite heart are o'er it;
> Go, read its legend—"Trust in God,"
>   On Faith's white stones before it.

> *The eyes of the Lord are upon the righteous, and his ears are open unto their cry.*—Psalm 34:15

How we should be continually uttering the memory of His great goodness!

> Marvelous grace of our loving Lord,
>   Grace that exceeds our sin and our guilt,
> Yonder on Calvary's mount outpoured,
>   There where the blood of the Lamb was spilt.
>
> Sin and despair like the sea waves cold,
>   Threaten the soul with infinite loss;
> Grace that is greater, yes, grace untold,
>   Points to the Refuge, the Mighty Cross.
>
> Dark is the stain that we cannot hide,
>   What can avail to wash it away?
> Look, there is flowing a crimson tide;
>   Whiter than snow you may be today.
>
> Marvelous, infinite, matchless grace,
>   Freely bestowed on all who believe;
> You that are longing to see His face,
>   Will you this moment His grace receive?

To judge of the importance of a remedy, it is necessary to know the malignity of the disease! To ascertain the claims of a benefactor to our gratitude and love, it is necessary for us to know the evils from which he delivers us. Everything turns upon this. If sin be our worst enemy, it is easy to prove that He who saves us from it is our best friend. The medicine is for the diseased; the quickening is for the dead! The pardon is for the guilty; the liberation is for those who are bound. The opening of the eyes is for those who are blind; the cleansing is for the filthy.

Rejoice, if in Christ you have trusted, that

X — IN CHRIST THROUGH WHOM IS THIS GRACE WE
    HAVE VICTORY OVER SIN AND SINNING.

"Thanks be unto God who giveth us the victory through our Lord Jesus Christ." Don't forget that Jesus was tempted in all points like as we are. In vain Satan attacked Him with all temptations, but Jesus had not tinder in Him to give fire to those matches.

Hereafter I will not talk much with you: for the prince of this world cometh, and hath nothing in me.—JOHN 14:30

Jesus never had any consciousness of sin. And Jesus was always talking about sin. He had eyes to see sin everywhere. He prayed, "Father, forgive *them*." But never did He pray, "Forgive *me*." There is not a trace in Christ of any scar healed. In all His life no trace of regret or remorse — no word of penitence, nor any sign of shame. "In him was no sin" (I John 3:5).

"There is therefore *now* no condemnation to them that are in Christ Jesus." So you see we do not have to wait until we die to get deliverance. We do not have to wait until we die to get the yoke of bondage broken. We do not have to wait until we die to be delivered from the things that bind and blind and grind. Thank God we can have deliverance *now*.

In loving kindness Jesus came
My soul in mercy to reclaim,
And from the depths of sin and shame
Through grace He lifted me.

He called me long before I heard,
Before my sinful heart was stirred,
But when I took Him at His word,
Forgiv'n He lifted me.

From sinking sand He lifted me,
With tender hand He lifted me,
From shades of night to plains of light,
O praise His name, He lifted me.

If you will yield yourself up to His divine working, the Lord will alter your nature—*now*. He will subdue the old nature—*now*. He will breathe new life into you—*now*. Put your trust in the Lord Jesus—now—and now, right now; immediately He will take away the stony heart, and give you a heart of flesh. Where everything was hard, everything will be tender — *now*. Where everything was vicious, everything will be virtuous—now. Where everything was tended downward, everything shall rise up with impetuous force—now. The lion of anger shall give place to the lamb of meekness—now. The raven of uncleanness shall fly before the dove of purity—now. The vile serpent of deceit shall be trodden under the heel of truth—now.

> Amazing grace, how sweet the sound
>   That saved a wretch like me;
> I once was lost, but *now* am found—
>   Was blind, but now I see.

Maybe a thousand questions of your life you cannot answer now. But there is one question you can settle, independent of man, woman, angel, devil — and that is that you will be God's man, God's woman, *now*, henceforth and forever.

The world wonders at the charge of the Light Brigade, immortalized by Tennyson. Only a few of the six hundred got back from the charge under Lord Cardigan, of the Muscovite guns; and all the havoc was done in twenty-five minutes. The charge beginning at ten minutes past eleven o'clock and closing at thirty-five minutes past eleven, and yet nothing left on the field but dying and dead men, dying and dead horses. But a smaller proportion of the men and women who go into the battle of life come out unwounded. The slaughter has been and will be terrific, and we all need God, and we need Him now. We need Him all the time. Let me say there is a new woman, as there is a new man, and that is the regenerated woman made such by the ransacking, transforming, upbuilding, triumphant power of the Spirit who is so superior to all other spirits that He has been called for ages the Holy Spirit. Quicker than wheel ever turned on its axle; quicker than fleetest hoof ever struck the pavement; quicker than zig-zag lightning ever dropped down the sky, the ransoming power I speak of will revolutionize your entire nature. Then you can start out on a voyage of life, defying both calm and cyclone, saying with Dean Alford:

> One who has known in storms to sail
>   I have on board;
> Above the roaring of the gale
>   I hear my Lord.
> He holds me when the billows smile;
>   I shall not fall;
> If short 'tis sharp, if long 'tis light;
>   He tempers all.

CHAPTER THREE

THE INFLUENCE OF A CHRISTIAN HOME

As for me and my house, we will serve the Lord.
                                        —JOSHUA 24:15
Let them learn first to show piety at home.
                                        —I TIMOTHY 5:4

I — WONDER OF THE HOME

GOD made Adam out of the dust of the ground and breathed into his body the breath of life. Thus Adam became a living soul. Before his Maker he stood innocent and unspotted. But with all his glory, power and pleasure, Adam was lonely, solitary. God saw that amid all this creative works, which He pronounced good, that it was not good for man to be alone. Woman was, therefore, created — made from Adam's rib. She was brought to man — and there, in the sinless garden, they were united in holy wedlock. Upon this pure and primal pair God bestowed His divine blessing. They were commanded to found a worthy race, subdue the earth into utility, and rule the world for God. Thus God established the home as a unit of society. Centuries before there was a state, school, or church, there were homes instituted by God as places where men and women should live together in love and in happiness, where children should be born and reared. This fellow-

ship of married love and the home which it builds is
God's supreme gift to man and the safeguard of civilization. The matter of supreme importance to the nation
is not the schools, not the state, not the national government, but homes which produce a noble civilization.

The home may be made in a tent, a rented house, an
apartment, a mansion, a cabin. The home, as one has
said, is a fold that shelters the family from the wolves
of lust, strife, unbelief — a harbor in which souls
anchor and abide secure from the storms of doubt and
carnal stress that are without — a fortress from whose
citadel the armed forces of love, truth, chastity, go
forth to bless the world — a sanctuary in which faith
builds an altar, opens the door of prayer, and yields
life and life's destiny to God. Moreover, a Christian
home is an ante-room to heaven where husband and
wife "submit themselves one to another in the fear of
God," where parents rear their children in God's nur-
ture and admonition, where children obey their parents,
where God's Word has a place, where the Sabbath rolls
in tender blessing over the threshold — a field where
love grows its orchard of most delicious fruits. Most
of what heaven is, our homes may be if we serve God
and give Christ's religion the main track and not the
sidetrack. A church within a church, a republic within a
republic, a world within a world, a kingdom within a
kingdom is spelled in four letters — H O M E. If things
go right there, they go right everywhere. The door-
sills of homes are the foundations of church and state.
No man ever gets higher than his own garret nor lower
than his own cellar. The highest house of congress
is the domestic circle. The rocking-chair in a Christian
nursery is higher than a throne. It is not too much to
say that though George Washington commanded the

forces of the United States, Mary Washington commanded George. Chrysostom's mother sharpened his
pen for him and kindled unquenchable spiritual fires
in his heart. If a man should start out to run seventy
years in a straight line, he could not get from under the
shadow of his own mantel-piece. If the modern mother
throws the cares of her household into a servant's lap
and spends the afternoons and nights at clubs, operas,
theaters, she may clothe her children with satins and
laces that would confound a French milliner, but her
children are orphans. And there are too many orphans
today.

Home implies a man who works, a woman who is
good, a child who is taught. Only the man who works
is a good citizen, for he assumes his due responsibility
and his veins are the veins of blessing to any land.
Only the woman who is good is fit for mothering—
and the world needs mothers more than statesmen, poets,
scientists or professors. Only the child who is taught is
reared to be a blessing.

Do you want to reform society? Don't mount the
soap-box and give circumlocutory cycles of oratorical
sonority. Go home! Don't turn columnist. Go home!
No movement will move unless it moves there. No
reform unless it originates there. No law stands unless
it is favored there. No religion prospers unless it is
usable there. A real democracy, after all, is a cluster
of homes, not individuals. What institution irritates the
apostles of unrest? What institution disgusts the can-
tankerous radical? What institution confuses the wild
purposes of the grouch propagandist? The home! The
home is the heart of civilization. A wise teacher of the
ancient world said: "give me a single domestic grace
and I will turn it into one hundred public virtues." The

home is like a reservoir pouring water into every avenue in moral life, in social life, in political life, in all life. If there are not enough moral principles to make the family adhere, there will not be enough political principles to make the state adhere. The same storm that upsets the ship in which the family sails will sink the frigate of the Constitution. The door of the home is the best fortress. Household utensils are the best artillery against evil invasions.

II — THE HOME IS A NEGLECTED AGENCY OF GOD TODAY

This is to say that there is a damaging if not damning decline in home piety and home spirituality. There is a decline of family religion that predicts disaster among us. With the decay of our home life will come the decay of civilization. The home is where the alphabet of the gospel is first learned; and when our homes become the generators of spiritual influences, we shall witness an infusion of new power in the life of the churches. One of our great handicaps in church life today is the indifference of many homes to spiritual values.

There are evidences that the influence of the home is less strong on the constructive side than in earlier days. The home has experienced difficulty in keeping pace with alternative diversions, in consequence of which the parent-child relationship is threatened. The influence of the home is foundational and primary. So obvious is this fact that it seems unnecessary to labor the point. The defective home is the primary cause of prostitution, drunkenness, idleness, and all the evils and isms that would cause us to hand down our blood-bequeathed legacies reduced in quality and in quantity.

The purification and power of our national life is dependent upon the home. The over-production of spiritual pygmies today is traceable to the absence of great homes. Great homes are necessary to produce great men, whether that home be a cabin on the hill, a tent by the river brink, a cottage by the roadside, a mansion on the boulevard, or a farmhouse amid far-reaching acres. In Christian households is the hope of America.

We have education today, but education has not eliminated crime, even though our great educational leaders of the last century promised the abolishment of crime if only we would educate — build schools, support them, and pass compulsory attendance laws for all children. These well-intentioned men said then that in a generation crime would be a thing of the past. We did all this — but crime is still with us. On unimpeachable authority, we have the cost of crime in this country — fifteen billions of dollars — over-topping by some billions a year all the money spent for educational, religious and charitable purposes put together. As Livy said of his day, "Our vices have risen to so great a height that we can endure neither the burden of them nor the sharpness of their remedy."

The world we live in contains all the elements of Joshua's world — the same gods beckon and the same forces prevail. The conscienceless profiteer inflames the feeling of fear and hate in the name of patriotism. The literary camp-followers of the new psychology flatter men's passions in the name of science. Self-labeled scholarship summons the Bible to appear at the bar of human reason. The hucksters of finance tease with their ballyhoo in the name of security. The alternatives again spread before us — the inevitable option — God or Mammon, Jesus or Venus. Ultimately, like the spider, we weave the web of our destiny out of the stuff of our own being.

III — THE HOME FUNCTIONS FOR GOD AND CIVILIZATION WHEN—

1. *There is Parental Authority.*

Lawlessness in the nation gets its start by the fireside. The child that respects not the authority of parents will not respect the authority of God and "the powers that be" when he comes to manhood. Many children are ruined by the over-indulgence of a pair of easy-going, church-complacent parents. God said about Abraham, "For I know him, that he will command his children and his household after him, and they shall keep the way of the Lord." Today, parental authority, as some wit has said, has not disappeared, but has only changed hands. Children have taken it over, he says.

I was visiting once in a home where the little boy of the home, about six or seven years of age, insisted on picking the kitten of the house up by the tail. The kitten squirmed and squalled. The mother said, "Put the kitten down!" But he did not do so. She said: "If you don't put the kitten down, I'll switch you!" But he held onto the kitten as though it were a purse with many shining dollars in it. Then she said: "If you don't put the kitten down, the preacher will bite you!" But he didn't put the kitten down—and I didn't bite the little chap. But I left, saying to myself, "A criminal career is being started in that home."

Will Durant, famous poet and philosopher, speaking in Knoxville, Tennessee, urged the revival of parental authority as the remedy for moral decay today. He said, "All character in America has been generated in the countryside where parental authority is strong and has died in the cities where parental authority is weak. While the youth of America is faced with great problems and probably being led to the abysses and horrors of war, it is eating gold fish and reading smutty stories. Almost fifty percent of the next generation is growing up without that implantation of decency."

Recently I spoke in Chicago. While there I read from the Chicago Tribune a case of parental buck-passing on youths' scandals. A nasty case of juvenile immorality in the Morton High School was brought up. The high school students were involved in scandal and hell-raising. There, as is a frequent tendency everywhere, was a tendency to call the school board or the teacher to account. They forgot that the principal responsibility for the conduct of their children rests in their parents— and not with the school teachers. Judge Bicek summoned forty fathers in the Juvenile Court and charged them with this responsibility. Their sons were in trouble—some started on criminal careers. The Judge said: "Parental neglect causes ninety percent of our juvenile cases." Then he said that parents are legally responsible for civil damages due to their children. "They might well also be placed in the dock beside children charged with criminal offenses, not to be tried for those offenses, but to be tried to ascertain whether their negligence contributed to these moral offenses."

Mr. L. E. Thomas, boys' secretary of the Y.M.C.A. in Memphis, Tennessee, told me of some boys who were caught stealing golf balls at the "Stop and Sock" Golf Club. The fathers and mothers of these boys called Mr. Thomas in to counsel with him as to what to do with these boys. Can you imagine the old-fashioned fathers and mothers of a generation past doing a thing like that? My old father—deacon for forty-two years in a

Baptist church—would have done no such absurd thing. Nor my mother. Nor yours. Parents of years gone by would have done a little "socking and stopping" on their own account. I think we need some old-fashioned, Bible-loving, God-fearing, children-bearing, and children-ruling fathers and mothers who "command their children after them." Too many children, born of Godless parents, are more damned into the world than born into it.

2. *We must have Christian experience and influence.*

Too many so-called homes are mere lunch counters with lodging quarters attached — places where children stay while the automobile is being fixed or when the movies are not running. Many children do not have a real chance to get acquainted with their parents nor parents with their children.

Out of one hundred and twenty ministers who were addressed in a western state, one hundred said that Christian influence in the home had much to do with their conversion and service in the ministry. A large proportion of young people who recently joined a certain church on profession of faith made claim that the influence of their homes turned them to think on the way of salvation and eternal life. But Tom Paine said, "I was an infidel before I was five years old." And Lord Byron, marvelous poet that he was, debauchee that he was, mistreated by his mother when he was a crippled child, said, "Untrained in youth my heart to tame, my springs of life were poisoned."

Not just Sunday religion do we need, not just company religion where we are better to visitors in our homes than to loved ones with whom we live. Not just pleasant day piety, but piety for old black Friday and blue Monday, and worrisome Wednesday, and trying Tuesday, and tribulation Thursday, and Satanic Saturday. Only in this way can homes build character.

William Lyon Phelps, Bible and English teacher and great Christian, recently said, "I am extremely grateful to my parents for the religious and spiritual training they gave me. Every day of my life I am grateful. I would rather belong to the church than to any other organization, society or club. I would rather be a church member than to receive any honor in the world. The hardest task in the world is the bringing up of children, and the chief reason is that example is so much more important than precept." Can parents lie about a child's age and teach it truthfulness? Can parents receive too much change and keep that change and expect the child to be honest? Can parents tell "little white lies" and expect their children to tell the truth? Can parents refuse to pray and expect to have prayerful children? Can parents habitually absent themselves from church and expect their children to love and properly evaluate the church?

3. *There must be tongue rule in the home.*

"If any man among you seem to be religious, and bridleth not his tongue, but deceiveth his own heart, that man's religion is vain." If people do not rule their tongues in the homes, happiness lies stark dead on the hearthstone. When the husband's position as head of the household is maintained by loudness of voice, strength of arm, or fire of temper, the republic of domestic bliss has become a despotism that neither God nor man can abide. And when the wife, instead of revering her husband, is always wrangling or railing at him, it makes doleful living — makes him long for a lodge in some vast wilderness—and makes much matrimonial milk turn to clabber. Spurgeon once said, "It must be a good thing when such women are hoarse; and it is a pity that they have not as many blisters on their tongues as they have teeth in their jaws." God save us from husbands and wives who are angels in the street, saints in the church, devils in the home. I have never tasted these bitter herbs in my own life, but I pity from my heart those who have this every day of their life. "How," Spurgeon asks, "would you like a world where all the skies hurtled with storms and all seas are storm-ridden and all mountain streams are raving mad, frothing at the mouth with mud foam, with simoons blowing among the hills — with never a lark's carol or a water fowl's splash, but only a bear's bark, a panther's scream, a wolf's howl, a boar's grunt, a mad bull's bellow?"

Spiritually dark homes make bad boys and turn bad girls into bad women. I fear that if musicians were as blundering in the musical realm as we are in showing spiritual piety in the home, what a mournful monotony of jangling disharmony our musical efforts would be! If bankers were as thoughtless in handling funds as many are in the home, they would be forced to wear clothes not found in a haberdasher's shop, and to talk to visitors through a wire screen. If doctors were as careless in their practice of medicine as many of us are in our manifestations of a Christ-like spirit in the home, there would be large additions to all our cemeteries. Let us learn first to show piety at home—hourly, daily, weekly, monthly, yearly — all the time.

4. *Love must be professed and possessed.*

Without love no amount of luxurious furnishing can make a happy home. With love a one-room cabin or a two-room flat can be a home. Love is the chief luxury of any home. The real walls of the home are not made of wood or brick or stone, but of truth, love, loyalty. The real curtains of a home are not woven out of lace, but out of discretion. The real food of a home is not meat, not bread, but thoughtfulness and unselfishness. The real drink of a home is not wine, not water, not milk, but love which is both a food and an intoxicant. The real light in every home is not of electric lights by night nor of the sun by day, but of loyalty, love, courtesy — always in dear eyes shining, always in true hearts burning. The home is not a place where we lay off our clothes, but our cares — not a place where we are to shake fists and point critical fingers, but to bend knees in earnest prayer and to have the tongues of the just, more to be valued than choice silver.

A man's home is a real fortress in a warring world, where a woman buckles on his armor in the morning as he goes forth to the battles of the day and soothes his wounds when he comes home at night. But let us not forget that there is a vast difference in a house and a home. A house is built by human hands, but a home is built by human hearts. A house is built of such materials as carpenters use, but a home is built of invisible things of the spirit. Money buys the materials for a house, but the elements that go to make a home are priceless — far above rubies. A house may be destroyed, but no power, neither fire nor flood nor earthquake nor storms, can destroy a real home. Only one calamity can ruin a home — the death of love. When love dies, the home is in ruins — and all the material riches, successes and pleasures of living cannot supply what has been lost. The home is more than the house. It shelters it, but love makes a house into a home and love

works a miracle. Does not the house stand with sight-
less windows, unopened doors, hearthstone cold, spirit
dead until love comes in? Yes, tables, chairs, chests,
beds — are all stiff impersonal things that stand apart
until two people with love in their hearts take over this
house — and then these cold things warm up and become alive. Look at the dented cushion, the lighted
lamp beside the table, the books on the shelves. Listen
to the sound of voices. There seems to be a sort of a
breathing about them all. Love has taken charge. Only
love will keep orange blossoms from turning into lemon
peel. Only love that suffers long and is kind, vaunting
not itself, can keep wedding bells from turning into
tolling bells that announce the death of the home.

5. *We need breeding and rearing of men.*

A modern poet recently put it this way:

> You talk of your grade of cattle,
> And plan for a higher strain;
> You double the food of pasture,
> You heap up measures of grain,
> You draw on the wits of the nation,
> You better the barn and the pen,
> But what are you doing, my brothers,
> To better the breed of men?
>
> What of your boy? Have you measured
> His needs for the growing years?
> Does your mark as his sire in his features
> Mean less than your brand in your steers?
> Thoroughbred! That is your watchword,
> For stable, for pasture, for pen;
> But what is your word for the homestead?
> Answer, you breeders of men!

6. *Christ must be given a large place in the home.*

We have something of what that home would be when

we study the New Testament, for Paul gives us a picture of the domestic life of Spirit-filled believers.

> *Children, obey your parents in the Lord: for this is right. Honor thy father and mother; which is the first commandment with promise; that it may be well with thee, and thou mayest live long on the earth. And, ye fathers, provoke not your children to wrath: but bring them up in the nurture and admonition of the Lord.*—Eph. 6:1-4

That claims the attention of all children. "Wives, submit yourselves unto your own husbands as unto the Lord" (Eph. 5:22). "Husbands, love your wives, even as Christ also loved the church, and gave himself for it" (Eph. 5:25). "Walk in love as dear children." "Let them learn first to show piety at home."

In the home, if the mother is devoted to a life of amusement and dominated by the fashions of this world, the children conform to that pattern of character and conduct. If the father is more intent on accumulating money than on living a high and holy life, the children drink in his mammonistic spirit and imbibe his godless commercialism. On the other hand, if both parents are prayerful in spirit and exhale in their daily life the fragrance of piety, the children fall under that Christian spirit and derive their type of life from the pressure it brings to bear upon them.

Unfortunately for our country, multitudes of homes are as pagan as any found in heathen lands. Such godless homes hardly deserve the holy name of home at all. The house in which the parents and children live is little more than a place for lodging and feeding. To it they go as animals go to their shelter and their food from day to day, and of that the outcome is rank animalism in the form of human nature. Let us not forget that the home is the unit of Christian civilization — provided it is civilizing and Christianizing in its character. But many homes are not units of civilization; they are units of paganism and forces that damage all who live with them. When will we ever learn that it is better for children to be brought up amid some physical discomforts rather than to live in an atmosphere unfriendly to faith and unfavorable to spiritual religion?

We need to get back to God's standards for a Christian home as Christ would have us to maintain it. How we need to exalt the sacredness of the marriage tie! How we need to give Christ the throne, not the footstool in our homes! How we need to offer Him the whole house instead of the attic or the cellar! We need Christlike homes where the Bible is read daily, where prayer is made daily, where love is expressed daily, where the whole family attends church together, where conversation about the things of the kingdom of God is a rule rather than an exception, where the family income is tithed and taken to God's house, where God's law of piety and conduct is respected, where parents understand that children do not have to understand all the Bible to be saved. What child has to know about the laws of gravitation to learn to walk? What child has to know that there are seven colors in every ray of light in order to recognize its mother's face? What child has to know the velocity of sound waves in order to know its father's voice? When will the homes cease to handicap churches by telling children that they are not old enough to trust Christ? Did the children in the wilderness when they were snake-bitten have to die because they were too young to look on the brazen serpent on the pole? Must we tamely submit to the indifference of parents and try to make a puzzle out of

God's plan of salvation and thus see our boys and girls
go the way to eternal doom and death? God forbid!
If many of our children were as dumb in their books
at school as many parents seem to believe they
are as to the plan of salvation, many children would
get their high school diplomas at forty and fifty years of
age. Let us give Christ the center in all of our homes—
attics, cellars, kitchens, bedrooms, closets, parlors, all.
Then most of what heaven is our homes will be to the
glory of God and the happiness of human families. I
put on your heart what Grace Noll Crowell wrote as to
our homes:

> Here Christ shall come and here He shall abide;
>   Our table shall be set for our great guest—
> Our lamps be lit, our hearts be warm and wide;
>   And here He shall find shelter, food, and rest.
>
> And He will talk with us beside our fire,
>   And He will walk with us through every task.
> We can confide every hope and every desire,
>   No question be too great or small to ask.
>
> Because He lives with us, is one of us,
>   We shall take care no evil shall be heard—
> Because His ways are kind and courteous,
>   We shall watch our ways in every spoken word.
>
> This is our new house. Lord, be Thou its head.
>   We gladly share its simple fare with Thee.
> Sit at our table, break and bless our bread—
>   And make us worthy of Thy company.

IV — THUS TRUSTING CHRIST, HONORING CHRIST, AND
     SERVING CHRIST — WE SHALL BE READY FOR
     THE HEAVENLY HOME.

What Mary and Martha said to Jesus, we could say
concerning homes that are just houses today —"Lord,
if thou hadst been here, my brother had not died."

There are countless homes that have become domestic tombs built by no other cause than this — Christless hearts that walk a Christless way. Domestic skeletons over our land represent blighted and blasted homes; and these blighted and blasted homes represent husbands and wives who sincerely resolved to build and maintain a home, but later compromised on a *house*. Many young people have started out with the idea that a fine house and fine furnishings and fine social contacts and a fine bank account can assure a happy home. Journeying with this assumption, they inevitably find that fine carpets are thorny roads, that some fine social friends are fair weather friends, and that fine bank accounts have less value than they believed — and that when they have won the fine house and fine furnishings and fine shine in the social circle, they have no home to put in their house. They have sacrificed the things that make a home for a house. The chill of death is in the house. The fires of love have gone out. The darkness of the grave broods there. The grave clothes of the home that should have been in their house have been woven in the loom of ill temper, in the loom of selfishness, in the loom of wastefulness, in the loom of unfaithfulness, or in the loom of wrong emphasis. Often the luxury and self-indulgence which parents bestow exclude "the atmospheric pressure of godliness." Only the Lord of life can bring these dead homes back to life. The Lord who has power over death and the grave. Jesus rebuked the people of His day by asking, "Is not the life more than the food that sustains it?" "Is not the body more than the clothing that covers it?" We might justifiably ask today, "Is not the home more than the house that shelters it?" Only as we get and have and hold the truth that Jesus should have and hold reign in our lives and homes will we be ready for abundant entrance into the heavenly home — when the summons shall come "to join that innumerable caravan." Only in this way can we stand before Him in that solemn and glorious hour unashamed and unafraid.

Some day we must leave our earthly homes — for death, whose only palace is a huge sepulchre, whose only pleasure fountains are the falling tears of the world, whose only laughter is a wail, whose only music is a sob of broken hearts, is busy. Some day, if the Lord Jesus lingers longer, you and I will have to stand face to face with the black door of death and deal with death — the one sanctity that all men respect, the one gesture that melts the hardest, the one awe that appalls the impious, the one stroke of common sense that annihilates our folly, the one preacher of righteousness and justice and nobility whose lips cannot be stilled.

I thank God that when we are summoned to go from our earthly homes that there is a heavenly home already prepared for those who love Him and that home is the most beautiful place that the wisdom of God could conceive and the power of God could prepare. Oh, to be at home with him! Home — with its music! Home— with beauty for our eyes! Home — with joy for our hearts! Home — with service for our hands! Home— with songs of praise for our mouths! Home — with testimony for our lips! Home — with worship for God!

Just here I am made to think of the scene set forth in the Revelation:

> *After this I beheld, and, lo, a great multitude, which no man could number, of all nations, and kindreds, and people, and tongues, stood before the throne, and before the Lamb, clothed with white robes, and palms in their hands; and cried with a loud voice, saying, Salvation to our God which sitteth upon the*

throne, and unto the Lamb. And one of the elders answered, saying unto me, What are these which are arrayed in white robes, and whence came they? And I said unto him, Sir, thou knowest. And he said to me, These are they which came out of great tribulation, and have washed their robes, and made them white in the blood of the Lamb. Therefore are they before the throne of God, and serve him day and night in his temple: and he that sitteth on the throne shall dwell among them. They shall hunger no more, neither thirst any more; neither shall the sun light on them, nor any heat. For the Lamb which is in the midst of the throne shall feed them, and shall lead them unto the living fountains of waters: and God shall wipe away all tears from their eyes.

—REVELATION 7: 9-10, 13-17

Let us so live that when our summons shall come to leave our earthly homes we can calmly and trustfully say what the poet said:

> Adieu, sweet friends, I have waited long,
> To hear the message that calls me home;
> And now it comes like a low sweet song,
> Of welcome over the river's foam;
> And my heart shall ache and my feet shall roam—
> No more, no more; I'm going home.
>
> Home! Where no storm, where no tempest raves
> In the light of the calm eternal day;
> Where no willows weep over lonely graves,
> And the tears from our eyelids are kissed away,
> And my soul shall sigh and my feet shall roam—
> No more, no more; I'm going home.
>
> Friends will be there I have loved long ago—
> And joy like a river around me will flow.

So, in thought of that day when the pierced hands that opened to us the gates of grace shall open to us the gates of glory, let us profess and possess and manifest the religion of our Lord Jesus in our earthly homes.

CHAPTER FOUR

THE BIGNESS OF BARNABAS

*For he was a good man, and full of the Holy Ghost
and of faith: and much people was added unto the
Lord.*—ACTS 11:24

I — TRIBUTES

IN the Bible we find great tributes paid to men and
women who "served their day and generation by the
will of God." Of Abraham we read: "He was the
friend of God." Of Joseph: "A man in whom the Spirit
of God is." Of Moses: "He endured as seeing him
who is invisible." Of Enoch: "He had this testimony,
that he pleased God." Of Obadiah: "He feared the
Lord greatly in Ahab's house." Of Amaziah: "He offered himself willingly unto the Lord." Of Caleb: "He
followed the Lord fully." Of John the Baptist: "A man
sent from God." Of Dorcas: "A woman full of good
works and alms deeds which she did."

In literature and history we find praiseful tributes
paid to others whose brief day is over.

Of Lincoln, Markham wrote:

> The rectitude and patience of the rocks,
> The gladness of the wind that shakes the corn,
> The justice of the rain that loves all leaves,

> The pity of the snow that hides all scars,
> The loving kindness of the wayside well,
> The tolerance and equity of light.

Of Washington, Shannon wrote:

A man in whom the rugged grandeur of our mountains towered, in whom the patience of God's stars shone, in whom the noble rage of our seas sobbed, in whom the modesty of violets bloomed.

Of Gladstone, Abbott wrote:

In Christ his mighty intellect found anchorage,
In Christ his impetuous temper found restraint,
In Christ his versatile personality found fulfillment.

Of Pitt, Carroll said:

One such man in one thousand years is about all the world can produce.

Of Henry Grady, a news reporter wrote:

An animated aurora he, with all the variations of a sunset, and he managed in twenty minutes to bathe two antagonistic sections in fraternal light.

Of General Lee, Hill spoke:

He was a Caesar without his ambition, a Frederick without his tyranny, a Napoleon without his selfishness, a Washington without his reward—watchful as a Roman vestal, as submissive to law as Socrates, as grand in battle as Achilles.

Of Baxter, another wrote:

He was a pen in the hand of God.

Of Cromwell, one said:

He was a God-intoxicated man. He dipped his sword in heaven.

While these are only a few tributes paid by men to men, I doubt if any tribute is greater than that paid to Barnabas from the isolated island of Cyprus in the

Mediterranean! In Holy Writ, we read: "He was a good man, full of the Holy Ghost and of faith and many people were added to the Lord." Such could never be said of a little man — never of any man who thinks with provincialism or walks with the step of a dwarf. Never could that be written or spoken of any man who weighs less than sixteen ounces to the pound, who measures less than thirty-six inches to the yard, who strikes less than twelve for God. Never can this be said of any man who is less in the dark than in the light. But this is an adequate tribute to Barnabas, who was a suitable ambassador of Christ who, though rich, for our sakes became poor, that we, through his poverty, might become rich. A prophet, a teacher, an apostle, one of the foremost men of his day, Barnabas was a great figure in early Christian history.

II — Barnabas Was a Good Man — *"He was a good Man."*

This does not mean that he was a *sinless* man. Few claim that for themselves. Few claim that for others. The Bible claims that for no man — save Jesus, Who said: "Who convinceth me of sin?" The Bible, in statement after statement, in biography after biography, repudiates the claim of sinlessness or human perfection that any man might make for himself. Only of Jesus who was perfectly *human* can we say that he was a *perfect* human. Nevertheless, if people can say about us that we are brilliant or wealthy or brainy or strong or talented or politically powerful or famous or handsome or beautiful or popular or eloquent and, after all that, they cannot say of us that we are good, they have said nothing about us worth remembering. That prosaic and dull, but great virtue — a possession more to be desired than many things men treasure is the virtue of goodness. It should influence us as a stimulant, not as a bromicide — as a trumpet sounding reveille, not taps. When we hear that word "goodness" we should thrill. At its mention, our blood should run a bit faster, our pulses thrill, our hearts rejoice. We should eagerly sit up and lean forward attentively at every discussion of goodness. But — do we? We sometimes hear expressions such as these: "She is a *good* girl, but not a bit *pretty*, poor thing!" "He is a *good* fellow, but not at all *popular*—poor fellow!" Or, "He isn't much account and he will not work, but he is a *good* fellow." "He is not industrious and he likes his liquor once in a while, but after all, he is a *good* chap." And the garment fits about as well as Saul's armor fit the stripling— David. And such a statement carries about as much spiritual weight as a toy wagon could carry of scrap iron. And such a conception is about as appropriate as Goliath's sword for a manicure knife.

Men and women often-married, folks of genius, folks of athletic prowess, folks of spectacular stunts, famous folks, much-talked-about folks, politically powerful people, men of wealth — these folks and others in the same category, many folks are interested in, but *good* men and women who prefer a good name to great riches! Why bore us? And *if* we ourselves are praised for talent or popularity or achievement or success, we are pleased. But who feels that he is adequately complimented by being called *good*? Somebody has told us that the word "good" is a bit like the fellow who went down from Jerusalem to Jericho, having fallen among thieves who have stripped it of its raiment and have wounded it and departed — leaving it half dead. The same somebody, Dr. Chapple, I believe, says that the word "good" has a hospital odor about it and savors of plasters and poultices and invalid chairs — that the word's right hand has lost its cunning, that the word's tongue has lost its fire, that the word's cheeks are corpse-like in their paleness, seeming to be in the last stages of consumption.

What foolish ways we have of associating this word! We mate it with folks of utter insipidity — with "good-for-nothing" folks, passive folks whose conduct is harmless "like a wax figure in a show window," or with people no more spiritually aggressive than a wooden Indian in front of a cigar store — with folks who never made a mistake and, consequently, never made anything worthwhile. Why mate this word only with folks as swift to do good as a snail and as magnetic as a mummy — folks "faultlessly faultless, icily regular, splendidly null"? How sharp yet how true are the words of him who said: "Sometimes when folks feel called upon to clothe some colorless insipidity, some incarnate nonentity with some sort of adjective, they throw around the screwy shoulders the once-glorious robe 'good'." Such mating of the glorious word "good" shows as much wisdom as mating the nightingale with the crow — or the carrier pigeon with a flying fish.

Yet, despite the popular misconception and the widespread abuse that the word "good" has received, it still has the shoulders and strength of a Samson, the lifting power of a Hercules, and the carrying power of an Atlas. Never is it a word to cover up deformity, the glaring defect of a moral minus sign, the nothingness of vacancy. Never is it to be used to make littleness and idleness and immaculate do-nothingness to acquire the hue of positive virtues! Never!

The Holy Spirit has left us the record that Barnabas

was a good man. No authentic writing of this good man do we have. But, living in a day when they had no typewriters, no telegraph, no printing press, and no "best-seller" novels, he, who in his day was a living epistle read and known of all men, has written himself imperishably into the pages of church history, indelibly into the hearts of millions who love the Christ he loved. Fruitfully has he planted himself into the gardens of human hearts the world over, and all — by being a good man. His daily life was a sermon. I am sure his conversation left no bitterness. He had faults, I know, but he was always trying to correct them. He was free from the slavery of his passions. He loved God and people with his pocketbook as well as with his heart. And because he lived life so well and loved so greatly and sacrificed so freely, "much people" were added unto the Lord. Had he lived in our day, we could write of Barnabas the words written on the tomb of General Gordon of Khartum:

> He gave his intellect to the ignorant, his sympathies to the sad, his energies to right the wrong, his substance to the poor, his life to his country, his heart to God.

III — BARNABAS WAS FULL OF THE HOLY SPIRIT — *"Full of the Holy Ghost."*

Barnabas was a Spirit-filled, Spirit-possessed man. He had spiritual commerce with the invisible world. He had and held an intelligent residence in the unseen. Every hour of every day of his waking time he was a channel through which the divine became articulate. As the eye is made for light, the ear for sound, the mouth for taste, the hand for touch, so the body of man is made for the habitation of the Spirit. The release of human personality for the glory of God is thus realized, together with its direction and fulfillment. So Barnabas, the energy of the invisible Christ personalized in him, was "always bearing about in his body the dying of the Lord Jesus that the life also of Jesus might be made manifest in his body." Thus Barnabas was a living testimony to the fact that Christ was "raised up from the dead by the glory of the Father." The life which Barnabas lived was, and is, explained by the fact that Christ lived in him — looked through his eyes, spoke through his mouth, worked through his hands, bowed through his knees, carried burdens through his shoulders, walked through his feet, throbbed through his heart. "He gave witness (Barnabas did) with great power of the resurrection of Christ" — by his words and by his deeds, and often more by deeds than by words.

We are told that when Nansen started on his Arctic expedition he took with him a carrier pigeon, strong and fleet of wing. After two years — two years in the desolate Arctic regions — he one day wrote a tiny little message and tied it under the pigeon's wing, and let it loose to travel two thousand miles to Norway. And, oh! what miles! What desolation! Not a living creature! Ice, ice, ice, snow and death! But he took the trembling little bird and flung her up from the ship — up into the icy cold air! Three circles she made and then, straight as an arrow, she shot south; one thousand miles over ice — one thousand miles over the frozen wastes of ocean, and at last dropped into the lap of the explorer's wife. She knew by the arrival of the bird that it was all right in the dark night of the North.

Even as thus Mrs. Nansen knew her husband was alive in the frozen North, so people who knew Barnabas and knew how he lived could not doubt that Christ was alive. Barnabas, "full of the Holy Ghost," could say: "Christ liveth in me."

Today the Lord needs more men like Barnabas. For the Lord, who once had need of a colt for his triumphal procession, needs human beings to go for Him and to do His work. The Creator needs His creatures. Omnipotence needs finite weakness. Such is in His plan and purpose — just as the steam must have its cylinder, the river its channel, the electric current its conducting wire. God has power enough to "weigh the mountains in scales and the hills in a balance," but He needs human conductors. The divine logic runs: "All power is given unto ME in heaven and on earth. Go YE, therefore." Let us, therefore, go — remembering that full surrender by ourselves *to* God is the precursor of the full use of us *by* God.

IV — Barnabas Was a Man Full of Faith — *"Full of faith."*

He was a man who for God began a thing, the end of which he could not see at the beginning. That is faith. He was a man who would not doubt though all his ships came drifting home "with broken masts and tattered sails." His faith kept him strong in the assurance that "we never test the resources of God until we attempt the impossible." A man full of faith, his life was a life in which every power of the soul pays homage to the will of God, every faculty in trustful dependence on the unseen. Thus did Barnabas avoid the tragedy we often witness — the tragedy of being energetically active and yet spiritually ineffective.

Barnabas, full of faith, believed that no weapon formed against him or his purpose to serve could prosper. Barnabas, full of faith, believed that, though the days were dark and bitter, God's promises were sure— though skies should fall. He deserves a place along with all the heroes of faith who "subdued kingdoms, wrought righteousness, obtained promises . . . out of weakness were made strong, waxed valiant in fight, turned to flight the armies of the aliens" — with all who had "tired of cruel mockings and scourgings, yea, moreover of bonds and imprisonment . . . being destitute, tormented, afflicted." May we, thinking upon the faith of Barnabas, pray the hymn:

> My faith looks up to Thee,
> Thou Lamb of Calvary,
>   Saviour divine;
> Now hear me while I pray,
> Take all my guilt away,
> Oh, let me from this day
>   Be wholly Thine.

V — BARNABAS WAS ABUNDANTLY AND VOLUNTARILY SACRIFICIAL.

Reading and remembering what others have written of him, we learn that he has been called the man of the generous hand. He sold his property and gave it all to Christ. He not only gave ALL, but that all was a great deal! His home was in Cyprus and, though a Levite, he owned property. Originally the Levites owned no land (Numbers 18:20). But the case of Jeremiah (Jer. 33: 7-15) shows that the rule was not always strictly observed, for a Levite could buy or inherit a piece of land. But in the new Christian community, where most had little wealth, this Levitical irregularity may have stood in the way of influence of Barnabas. There was NO COMPULSION, but the voluntary surrender of ALL for the good of the WHOLE at once gave Barnabas a place of prominence and power in the Jerusalem church, to the envy of Ananias and Sapphira.

Barnabas was sound in the doctrine and practice of stewardship. Dr. George Truett says: "The man who is genuinely Christian in his attitude toward money will be Christian in every other relation of life." Mackey says: "Generosity is a sum in subtraction." Meaning, I take it, that the giving of money is to be labeled Christian according to what we have left— after our giving is done. The widow, whom Christ has placed high and conspicuously in His "hall of fame" gave more than all the others because she had nothing left. And I suppose, even now, weighing gifts on God's scales, the poor man's penny is oft more than the rich man's dollars. Not only with hymns, with prayers, with church attendance, but with his pocketbook did Barnabas love God — and the shadow of the Cross was on that pocketbook by day and by night.

Surely, remembering that every good and perfect gift cometh down from God with whom is "no variableness or shadow of turning," in the light of "the unspeakable gift" with which He has blessed our race, we are not willing to give unto God as a miser pays taxes. Surely, in the light of the lesser gifts of which our lives are full, in the light of Christian homes with their light and laughter and joy, in the light of our country, "a thought in the mind of God from all eternity," in the light of our blood-bequeathed legacies, in the light of many things which we can classify as blessings from above, we are stimulated to ask ourselves the question: "How much owest thou unto the Lord?"

And let us not forget that this abundant giving of Barnabas was voluntary. No "putting the screws" on him by someone else. No outside pressure to "head the subscription list." No conscription — no coercion— no compelling — no forcing! The only conscription he knew was the conscription of the need of the day. The only coercion he yielded to was the coercion of humanity's distress. The only compelling to which he surrendered himself and his powers was the compelling of the great desire of his heart to "be up and doing for God!"

VI — BARNABAS RISKED HIS LIFE FOR GOD.

Read that twenty-sixth verse of the fifteenth chapter of Acts. It draws you like a warm fire on a winter night.

Men that have hazarded their lives for the name of our Lord Jesus Christ.

It stirs you like a reveille trumpet with no uncertain sound. It pulls you out of complacency like a strong hand that draws you away from the edge of an abyss. It compels you and woos you like the sweet strains of an old harp under the skilled hand of a master. It shows us how Barnabas knew how to draw on his life, to give himself to danger, to "endure hardness as a good soldier of Jesus Christ." He knew how to live dangerously, to run risks, to hazard his very life for the Christ whom he loved.

Looking upon Barnabas, let us ask if we know how to give up comforts — for Christ, if we know how to "count all things but loss"— for Christ. Or do we love ease? And are we victims of the easy task? When God's bugles call to sharing His crucifixion, are we content to sit in easy chairs and wear soft slippers? Do we yearn for the fellowship of His suffering? Do we care to present our bodies a living sacrifice, holy, acceptable unto God, which is our reasonable service? Can we endure the persecution of criticism and the scourging of tongues and the stocks of ridicule? Do we know how to bear abuse for Christ? Have we yet learned that "we who live are always delivered unto death for Jesus' sake that the life also of Jesus might be made manifest in our mortal flesh"? Can we, like Bunyan say: "My marks and scars I carry with me to show that I have fought His battle well"? Or do we fail to "endure hardness as good soldiers of Jesus Christ"? Or — have we become victims of the easy track? Or, have we not learned to follow in the train of Barnabas who gladly put his life in peril for God — in a day when evil had many heads, many horns, many eyes — in a day when iniquity had a golden cup in her hand — in a day when force, fire and fury were the attributes of the antagonisms of wrong and error? Barnabas drew not back when opportunities came to put his very life in danger for Christ. Like Esther, who faced death that her people might live, Barnabas hazarded his life that people might know Christ and live.

It is said that Martin of Basel, a contemporary of Martin Luther, received the Lord Jesus even as Luther had received Him, and that he wrote his confession of faith in Christ and in that confession proved his love for and devotion to the Savior who had redeemed him. Then he pried a brick out of the wall and hid his confession between the brick and the mortar and returned the brick. It was not heard of for one hundred years, when it was accidentally discovered. Who knows anything of Martin of Basel? But Martin Luther, coming to his faith as he crawled his weary way up the Santa Scala in Rome, came to his feet for an open confession of Christ. Then there came a dangerous day when a friend of Luther said to him: "There are many cardinals and bishops at Worms, and they will burn your body to ashes as they did that of John Huss." Luther replied: "Although they should make a fire that should reach from Worms to Wittenberg, and that should flame up to heaven, in the Lord's name I would pass through it and appear before them."

How we need the spirit to live dangerously for Christ — to stand firmly erect while others are bowing and fawning for praise and power — to wear threadbare clothes in the cause of Christ (if need be) while others, pleasing men rather than God, dress in broadcloth — to remain in honest poverty when others grow rich by fraud — to do our duty in silence and obscurity and under criticism while others prosper and grow famous although neglecting sacred obligations —to be outvoted, beaten, laughed at, ridiculed, derided, misunderstood, misjudged — to be standing alone (if need be) with all the world against you, remembering that—

> They are slaves who dare not be in the right with two or three.

How we need in the work of Christ the spirit of Barnabas of old and the spirit of General Butler of recent years! When General Butler was sent with nine thousand men to quell the New York riots, he arrived in advance of his troops and found the streets thronged with an angry mob, which had already hanged several men to lamp-posts. Without waiting for his men, Butler went to the place where the crowd was most dense, overturned an ash barrel, stood upon it, and began: *"Delegates from Five Points, fiends of hell, you have murdered your superiors,"* and the bloodstained crowd quailed before the courageous words of a single man in a city which Mayor Fernando Wood could not restrain with the aid of police and militia.

As we remember the words of Jesus, "Behold, I send you forth as sheep in the midst of wolves" (Matt. 10:16) and "The time cometh when whosoever killeth you will think he doeth God service" (John 16:2), let us recall what Shakespeare said: "He is not worthy of the honeycomb who shuns the hive because bees have stings."

VII — Barnabas Courageously Championed the Cause of the Discredited.

What he did for Paul proves this. Strangely enough, the conversion of Saul of Tarsus was only a rumor in Jerusalem after three years had gone swiftly away. Saul had spent most of that three years in Arabia— studying the Old Testament Scriptures concerning the coming of the Messiah, the Savior. Now after he had been the bloodthirsty leader of the Pharisaic persecution in Jerusalem, Saul found that it was hard to live down the past — to erase the footprints made in Satan's service, "to restore any of the months the locusts had eaten," to plant figs where he had cultivated thorns, to make people whom he had bruised and beaten to believe in his balm.

But the record is that a strange convert had come to the disciples — the strangest ever seen, the strangest ever heard. His hands are red with Stephen's blood. One of the greatest enemies the church had ever had— once a ravening wolf in the midst of the sheep — once a fierce hawk among the doves — had returned from Damascus where he, breathing out slaughter, had gone on a tour of persecution. And he returns an enthusiastic disciple, loving the Christ he once hated, loving the people he once held in contempt, earnestly desiring to do good to those whom he had maltreated through persecution.

Now to visit Cephas, Saul had come (Gal. 1:18)— not to be inducted into his apostolic office. That authority he had received "not of men, neither by man, but by Jesus Christ and God the Father who raised him from the dead" (Gal. 1:1). But Saul, wishing to carry on his Gentile mission in harmony with the disciples, knowing there was much he could learn about the earthly life of the Lord Jesus from Simon Peter who had companied with Him and conversed with Him, "abode with him fifteen days." At this time no other apostles save James, the Lord's brother, and Barnabas and Peter, were in Jerusalem. And the record is:

> *And when Saul was come to Jerusalem, he assayed to join himself to the disciples: but they were all afraid of him, and believed not that he was a disciple.*
> —Acts 9:26

Paul found he could not erase the remembrance of him as quickly as the heat of the sun drives away a wisp of fog — that he could not bury the past with one spadefull — that he could not extinguish a conflagration with one bucket of water.

Though Paul, in Damascus, had preached boldly in the name of Jesus, he brought no letters of recommendation from the Christians in Damascus. They all were afraid that he might be a "wolf in sheep's clothing"— a devil in the livery of heaven. They gave him the deaf ear to his assertions that he was of "this way." They gave him the suspicious eye as he was visiting Peter — withheld the hand of fellowship. They gave him the cold shoulder as he assayed to join himself to them. They gave him criticism and fear; demanded that

Saul should furnish proof of his sincerity before he be received as a brother in Christ. It was a moment of awful crisis for Saul and for Christianity! It was a moment fraught with all the powers of disaster.

Then the record is:

> *But Barnabas took him, and brought him to the apostles, and declared unto them how he had seen the Lord in the way, and that He had spoken to him, and how he had preached boldly at Damascus in the name of Jesus. And he was with them coming in and going out of Jerusalem.*—ACTS 9: 27-28

Thus we see that Barnabas staked his all — his reputation, his life, his church which was dearer than life— on Paul's sincerity. He gave Saul the weight of his influence, which weight was like a mighty anchor to a ship tempest beaten. He gave him his hand, which hand was like a keen sword to one sorely pressed in battle. Had it not been for that warm and strong extended hand of Barnabas, Saul might have been chilled into obscurity or chilled into rolling marbles instead of removing mountains for God—made an Atlas, permitted only to carry a straw, a Hercules lifting only a bag of feathers,—his theological eagle made to do the work of a clucking hen. With the Sanhedrin looking on Saul as a renegade Jew, with the apostles fearing him as a hypocrite, Barnabas took him as a brother beloved— championing the cause of the discredited and distrusted.

We find, too, considering John Mark, how Barnabas shows his belief in the Gospel of the Second Chance. When Paul and Barnabas embarked on their first missionary tour, what a great time it was for men! These two men presented Christ with fulness and power. How men would today flock to hear them! No distance would be too great to travel! No money too much to pay for that splendid privilege.

They took Mark! "And they had also John Mark as their attendant." The work of John Mark was to arrange for lodging, provide their food, interest people in the work by means of conversation, perhaps baptize the converts, for we know Paul baptized few.

> *So they, being sent forth by the Holy Ghost, departed unto Seleucia; and from thence they sailed to Cyprus. And when they were at Salamis, they preached the word of God in the synagogues of the Jews: and they had also John to their minister.*—ACTS 13: 4-5

And John Mark, journeying and voyaging with these two great men, witnessed wonders. In Cyprus, he saw one work of miraculous power — the blinding of Elymas, the sorcerer. He saw also one notable conversion — that of Sergius Paulus, the Roman proconsul. Every day in many ways Mark had convincing evidence of the divine origin of Christianity and of the conquering strength of the Holy Spirit. Few young men in the world's history have had so great an opportunity as John Mark.

Yet the young man's wonderful experience in Cyprus did not avail to keep him faithful. Neither did his affection for his Uncle Barnabas and his noble friend Paul. Maybe growing weary in well doing, or sickened by some fever, or discouraged, or homesick, or afraid to venture into the savage and perilous interior of Asia Minor, he quit the party. At Perga, the capital of Pamphylia, in the center of the Southern coast of Asia Minor, Mark left Paul and Barnabas — and went back to Jerusalem. Someone suggests as a reason that he disapproved of Paul's apparent purpose to work mainly

among the Gentiles. Anyway, whatever excuse or reason
Mark had, he forsook them.

Later on, in Antioch, a second missionary journey
was proposed by Paul.

> *And some days after Paul said unto Barnabas, Let*
> *us go again and visit our brethren in every city where*
> *we preached the word of the Lord, and see how they*
> *do. And Barnabas determined to take with them*
> *John, whose surname was Mark. But Paul thought*
> *not good to take him with them, who departed from*
> *them from Pamphylia, and went not with them to*
> *the work. And the contention was so sharp between*
> *them, that they departed asunder one from the other:*
> *and so Barnabas took Mark, and sailed unto Cyprus;*
> *And Paul chose Silas, and departed, being recom-*
> *mended by the brethren unto the grace of God.*
> —ACTS 15: 36-40

Barnabas, as we see, readily agreed to Paul's pro-
posal, but he suggested that they take Mark along. And
then Paul objected strenuously. Mark had played the
coward once at Perga. Paul said "no second chance!"
Barnabas said: "Though he failed one time, he need
not fail a second time!" Paul said: "I must have reliable men." "I will answer for him this time," Barnabas said. Paul said, "He that will not when he may,
when he will he shall have nay!"

Barnabas was not the man to say that John Mark
should be thrown to the scrap heap for his slip at
Perga. A man is entitled to a chance to come back.
Barnabas was one who believed that a man's worth is not
to be judged by how he failed on a certain occasion,
but by how he comes back after his failure — not by
how *low* he goes, but by how *high* he climbs back after
he goes *low*. You must not read the future of a man's
life down to the depths of a false step without giving

him a chance. You must not read a man's whole life
down to the level of a false day. And Barnabas was
right about Mark. When we hear Peter mention Mark
(I Peter 5:13) — and hear Paul mention Mark (Col.
4:10), and read what Paul writes to Timothy—II Timothy 4:11: "Take Mark and bring him with thee, for
he is profitable to me for the ministry," we say that a
radiant record shines behind the name of Barnabas who
permitted Mark to try again.

As Rossetti says:

> Once like a broken bow Mark sprang aside:
> Yet grace recalled him to a worthier course,
> To feeble hands and knees increasing force,
> Till God was magnified.

> And now a strong Evangelist, St. Mark
> Hath for his sign a lion in his strength;
> And through the stormy water's breadth and length
> He helps to steer God's Ark.

> Thus calls He sinners to be penitents,
> He kindles penitents to high desire,
> He mounts before them to the sphere of saints,
> And bids them come up higher.

VIII — Barnabas Was a Son of Consolation.

This we learn because of his work among the Greek
Christians in Antioch. We read:

> *Now they which were scattered abroad upon the per-*
> *secution that arose about Stephen, traveled as far as*
> *Phenice, and Cyprus, and Antioch, preaching the*
> *word to none but unto the Jews only. And some of*
> *them were men of Cyprus, and Cyrene, which, when*
> *they were come to Antioch, spake unto the Grecians,*
> *preaching the Lord Jesus. And the hand of the Lord*
> *was with them: and a great number believed, and*
> *turned unto the Lord.*—Acts 11: 19-21

Now this Antioch, its main street five miles long and paved with blocks of white marble, and lined with double colonnades of marble, was the seat of the Roman governor. Enriched by the caravans that came there from Persia and Asia, it was a city of great luxury and great wickedness. So notorious it was for its shameless corruption that Juvenal, the Satirist, characterized the degradation of Rome by saying: "The Syrian Orontes has flowed into the Tiber."

To this city where the church of Greek Christians was, Barnabas was sent as a "deputation of inquiry."

> *Then tidings of these things came unto the ears of the church which was in Jerusalem: and they sent forth Barnabas, that he should go as far as Antioch.*
> —ACTS 11:22

No man walking with the presumptuous step of a know-it-all or using any "bull-in-a-china-shop" method could wisely deal with the situation at Antioch. That situation, almost as difficult to handle as hot chestnuts in bare hands, required great tact. So the Jerusalem church showed its confidence in Barnabas and the esteem in which he was held by sending this good man as a committee of one to investigate conditions in Antioch— because, as Dr. Robertson says: "Barnabas himself was from Cyprus and may have known some of the brethren. A Hellenist, he could better appreciate their feelings toward these Greek Christians. A Levite, he could be trusted to understand their Hebrew prejudices. So to Antioch went Barnabas. Soon he saw that the work was due to the grace of God. In this he quietly rejoiced. Definite was his verdict. Reassuring was his verdict. He was glad that these simple souls had been thrust into such a ripe field and were gathering such a harvest.

> *Who, when he came, and had seen the grace of God,*
> *was glad, and exhorted them all, with purpose of*
> *heart they would cleave unto the Lord.*—ACTS 11:23

Then the record is:

> *Then departed Barnabas to Tarsus, for to seek Saul:*
> *And when he had found him, he brought him unto*
> *Antioch. And it came to pass, that a whole year*
> *they assembled themselves with the church, and*
> *taught much people. And the disciples were called*
> *Christians first in Antioch.*—ACTS 11: 25-26

"In Antioch he saw the same light in the faces of
the people that was in the faces of those who were
Spirit-baptized in Jerusalem — and he was able to let
facts sweep away prejudices." To these people he was
incarnated encouragement, embodied comfort, flesh-and-
blood consolation. A tongue of the learned had he—
to speak a word in season to him who was weary. From
the bondage of their self-depression, from the burden
of their self-despair, he delivered people. This good
man, pointing out the streaks of dawn, caused men to
"hear the bird's song within the voiceless egg," to catch
the perfume of flowers under the snow. He was in truth
a son of consolation! As Dr. Jowett says: "Barnabas
knew the old fruit when he saw it growing in a new
garden. He recognized the old tokens of grace, even
when they were revealed in strange conditions. There
is a great work for Barnabas nowadays, for everywhere God is revealing Himself in new and diverse
manners — and watchful, faithful men will love His
appearing."

IX — BARNABAS WAS SELF-FORGETFUL.

> *Then departed Barnabas to Tarsus for to seek Saul:*
> *And when he had found him, he brought him unto*
> *Antioch.*—ACTS 11: 25-26

There are tons of truth wrapped up in those simple words of Scripture. There are vast areas of glory there. These words are but a plain door that opens into the wonders of a palace — when we consider what events they lead us to consider. Up until the time when Barnabas brought Paul to Antioch, and up until the events in the isle of Paphos the order of their names is "Barnabas and Paul." But after that the order is changed to read "Paul and Barnabas." After Paul's sermon in Antioch of Pisidia we find Barnabas "playing second fiddle," not first fiddle. We read, "The religious proselytes followed Paul and Barnabas, who, speaking to them, persuaded them to continue in the grace of God" (Acts 13:43). Again: "Then Paul and Barnabas waxed bold" (Acts 13:36). And again, "But the Jews stirred up the devout and honorable women, and the chief men of the city, and raised persecution against Paul and Barnabas, and expelled them out of their coasts" (Acts 13:50).

But Barnabas had nothing of that spirit which Milton calls "jealousy, the injured lover's hell." He had in him no least bit of the jealousy which is, as the Bible says, "cruel as the grave" (Song of Solomon 8:6). He was free from the jealous and envious spirit which Thomson calls, "agony unmixed, incessant gall, corroding thought that blasts all Love's paradise." Barnabas had not in his heart's blood and life's blood one drop of that "base envy which withers at another's joy and hates the excellence it cannot reach." How little is any man who can have one shadow of grief or regret to pass over him by reason of anybody's bigness or greatness or popularity or success! And a man is possessed of much grace when it is known of him on earth and known of him in heaven that he is never jealous.

Paul said: "Love envieth not." Barnabas was so generously forgetful of himself that he had no room for envy in his heart. Before he went to Tarsus to get Paul to bring him to Antioch, he knew that Paul was the abler and stronger man — and that he, Barnabas, must inevitably yield first place to Paul. But caring only for the success of the work, with gracious spirit he allowed himself to be eclipsed by a younger luminary. Gradually his own light wanes while the brilliance of Paul comes to dazzle the eyes as immensely greater. Like John the Baptist, as the forerunner of Jesus, Barnabas, who introduced Paul to public place and public notice, was glad to see Paul increase. He had that love which envieth not. He was willing for the name of Barnabas to perish — if only the cause of Christ were furthered.

Barnabas played second fiddle, but he played it so well that the Kingdom of God made progress. He rode second in the Gospel chariot, but he did it with such humility and joy and gratitude until heaven will forever rejoice that he was "a good man, full of the Holy Ghost and of faith" and that, because of him, "much people were added unto the Lord."

CHAPTER FIVE

CHRIST THE DOOR TO SALVATION AND LIBERTY

*I am the door: by me if any man enter in, he shall
be saved, and shall go in and out, and find pasture.*
—John 10:9

JESUS, in the presence of a sinful woman snarled at
by some self-righteous scribes and Pharisees, said: "I
am the light of the world."

Think of what a bleak world this would be if never
a ray of sunshine broke through the darkness, if no
full moon ever glowed like a huge cameo pinned on
the breast of the sky, if no timid star ever winked
wooingly and brightly from the untroubled blue, if no
aurora borealis ever spread its silken skirts across the
garden of the stars — if we had to sleep and walk and
eat and love and work always in the dark. Jesus is
"the true light, which lighteth every man that cometh
into the world" (John 1:9). Republics, freedom of
thought, liberty of conscience, humanity of feeling for
the unfortunate, civic righteousness and natural righteousness — these which mean so much to us are here
only because Christ has been here.

Jesus on a day when "many of his disciples went
back and walked no more with him" (John 6:66), said,
"I am the bread of life."

Think of a world without bread! What a terrifying

sight starvation is! Yes — if it be a gasping baby tugging at a mother's empty breast or gray old folks to whom a crust is a feast. Yes — whether it be a colossal spectacle spread across the high plateau of Armenia or the bleak steppes of Russia, or whether we come upon it in the tenderly kept chamber of the invalid whose malnutrition no longer permits nourishment to be taken. Think of this world without bread and you get some idea of how necessary Jesus knew Himself to be to the life of the world. And when Jesus declared Himself to be the bread of life, He claimed to be as necessary and essential to the spiritual life of mankind as bread to the physical life.

Jesus once, "in the last day, that great day of the feast, stood and cried, saying, if any man thirst, let him come unto me and drink" (John 7:37).

Think how great is the torture of thirst — when even muddy drops are to parched mouths as rains to drouth-smitten gardens. What a relief is a spring in the desert! What a comfort is a pool in the wilderness! What music to the thirsty is the bubbling fountain, the babbling of a brook! A world without water is something like the world without Christ! The life without Christ! Jesus is just as essential to spiritual life as water for the body.

Jesus, at an hour when the shadow of the cross loomed darkly near, said: "I am the true vine" (John 15:1). And again: "I am the vine, ye are the branches: He that abideth in me, and I in him, the same bringeth forth much fruit: for without me ye can do nothing" (John 15:5).

Jesus is the center. From Him is to come spiritual life — its growth, its very nature, its productiveness, its beauty. And any preaching that has not Christ as center is not preaching when measured by God's standards. Any work done for God without Christ as the center is not Christian service. Any prayer without Christ as the center is not Christian prayer. Any giving without Christ as the motive is not Christian giving.

Jesus, on a day when He asked a blind man to wash his clay-anointed eyes and the blind man "went his way therefore and washed and came seeing" (John 9:7), was beset by His enemies. He said: "I am the good shepherd." In these words, Jesus shows us that He is guidance for us. It calls to mind Jesus' thoughtful and detailed provision for the needs of life — a reaffirmation of the promise in the Old Testament, so beautifully expressed in Isaiah 40:11:

> He shall feed his flock like a shepherd: he shall gather the lambs with his arm, and carry them in his bosom, and shall gently lead those that are with young.

Jesus, one drear day when the hearts of two sisters were desolate, said: "I am the resurrection and the life" (John 11:25).

Can you imagine what a desolation the natural world would be if the bleakness of winter never was broken by the coming of spring? If spring's trumpet, fashioned of sod and sunshine and sky, never sounded reveille at Nature's tomb? If never the bluebird flew by with the sky on his back? If never the bee sang his solo from the honied choirloft of blossom? If never the peach trees put on their pink petticoats? If you can imagine what desolation if there was death everywhere — until there was no need longer and no room longer for hearse and coffin and grave, you can well understand what a life is, what a home is, what an educational system is, what a world is without Christ.

Jesus, on a day when the lightning of hate from the thunder clouds of His enemies' wrath against Him was loosed, said: "I am the door: by me if any man enter in, he shall be saved, and shall go in and out, and find pasture" (John 10:9).

When He said this, He spoke of Himself as entrance and exit. What a strange world this would be if there were no entrance for the ploughshare into the soil, no entrance for miner's pick into the bowels of the earth, no entrance for fisherman's ship and net into the sea, no entrance for knowledge into human minds, no entrance into our homes, no entrance into the mysteries of nature, no entrance into the resources of God. And what a sad world this would be if there were no exit from darkness to light, from despair to hope, from sickness to health, from sorrow to joy! Now Jesus taught how essential He is to life, whether it be a thing of entrance or exit, when He said: "I am the door."

So we see that Jesus is

I — The Person of the Gospel — "*I.*"

"I," Jesus. Jesus — pre-existent and virgin-born. Jesus — human and divine. Jesus — riven, risen, ruling, returning. Jesus — in whom the fulness of the Godhead resides. Jesus — the image of the invisible God. Jesus, who illustrated in His daily life every doctrine of His heavenly mind. Jesus, who ever held up before mankind representative manhood gloriously conformed to the will of God. Jesus, whose face was incarnate sympathy, whose hand was friendship's symbol, whose eye was liquid sympathy for every human sorrow. Jesus, Son of the Father's love, "in whom we have redemption through His blood, even the forgiveness of sins" (Col. 1:14). Jesus, the first in dignity of all creation, for He created all the positions of dignity in the heavens and on the earth — the thrones, the lordships, the principalities, the powers. "Of him, and through him, and unto him are all things."

Dr. James A. Francis once wrote: "Jesus Christ is the explanation of human history, and no man, no matter how great his intellectual ability, has ever been able to find an adequate explanation of human history with Jesus left out. Take Jesus of Nazareth out of history, and the history of this world becomes the cruelest joke ever perpetrated by a demon; put Him in His proper place at the center of history, and before He gets through He will brighten the fields of earth with such a harvest of grace, and whiten the fields of heaven with such a harvest of glory, as will abundantly justify the ways of God."

Jesus explains all things. If you have a perplexity in your mind, take it to Jesus. He will solve it. If you are held by a fear, take it to Jesus and He will conquer it. If you are conquered by the noise and tumult around you, go to Jesus — and you will find peace. If you are weighed down by your past sins, take them to Jesus — and the burden will fall off. If you are lonely, go to Jesus — and He will give you the most glorious comradeship. He is the exit from bondage, sorrow and night and the door into freedom, gladness and light. He is the exit from the depths of ruin untold and the entrance into the peace of God's sheltering fold.

And considering Jesus, we learn of

II — THE PLAINNESS OF THE GOSPEL — *"The Door."*

The door! And not a door to which no one can approach and to which only "the high and mighty" have

the key. Not a door where kings and the rich are
welcomed and where the poor and beggars are for-
bidden. But a door where "whosoever will may come"
and where whosoever *believeth* may enter. "Him that
cometh unto me I will in no wise cast out." A door!
Not a door with puzzling locks and mysterious combinations. Not a door with labyrinthine intricacies.
Nobody needs to perform acrobatic stunts to enter. No
tight rope walking required to enter. No twisting and
turning to find the door and to enter therein. The way to
and entrance through that door is no "ferris-wheel"
affair. No translation of some foreign language, no
chemical analysis, no solving some algebraic problem,
no digging one's way through a hedge — not one of
these is required. But the way is *so* plain and the door
bright with such welcome glory and beauty. As plain
as Paul set it forth in the Philippi jail when he said:
"Believe on the Lord Jesus Christ and thou shalt be
saved" (Acts 16:31).

One does not have to know all about the laws of
gravitation to know how to walk. One does not have
to know there are seven colors in a ray of light and
that light vibrations are vertical and move one million times faster than the vibrations of air, to recognize
a loved one's face. One does not have to understand all
about the processes of digestion to eat a meal. One
does not have to know a definition for every word in
the dictionary to know how to make known a want to a
friend. One does not have to know all about psychology
and physiology to know how to sleep; does not have to
know all about the construction of the ear and that the
ear is capable of catching seventy-six thousand, two
hundred vibrations per second to know a loved one's
voice. Nor does one have to know and understand all

things in the Bible to be saved. But he *must* believe.
The Bible is always very definite and reassuring on that
point. A blind man cannot see. We know that. But we
know he can believe. A deaf man cannot hear. No boom
of thunder, no whisper of zephyr are his. We know
that. But we know he can *believe*. Many people cannot give a definition of a parallelepipedon. We know
that. But we know that they can *believe*. Cripples
cannot win hurdle races when in contest with the swift
of foot. We know that. But we know they can *believe*.

The plainness of the Gospel plan is seen in the words
"whosoever *will*." Not "whosoever *worketh*," because it
is *"not* by works of righteousness that we have done."
Not "whosoever hath good intentions," for mere good
intentions are but paper boats on a stormy sea. Not
"whosoever admireth Christ," for many admire Him as
a historical character who have never accepted Him as
Savior from sin. Not "whosoever acquiesces in all the
praise given Jesus," for many acknowledge He is worthy
of praise who have never opened to Him who "knock-
eth at the fast-closed door." Not "whosoever hath merit
in himself," for in the best of us is no good thing at
all that can cause us to deserve salvation. But "whosoever *believeth*." "He that *believeth* on him is not con-
demned" (John 3:18). "He that *believeth* on the Son
hath everlasting life" (John 3:36).

> *Verily, verily, I say unto you, he that heareth my
> word, and believeth on him that sent me, hath ever-
> lasting life, and shall not come into condemnation;
> but is passed from death unto life.*—JOHN 5:24

> *And they said, Believe on the Lord Jesus Christ, and
> thou shalt be saved, and thy house.*—ACTS 16:31

> *But now the righteousness of God without the law is
> manifested, being witnessed by the law and the*

> *prophets; even the righteousness of God, which is by
> faith of Jesus Christ unto all and upon all them that
> believe: for there is no difference.*—ROMANS 3: 21-22

And learning of Jesus, we find

III — THE PATHWAY OF THE GOSPEL — *"By me."*

"I am the *way.*" "No man cometh unto the Father
but by me." "I am the door of the fold; he that goeth
up any other way, the same is a thief and a robber."
"There is none other name given under heaven among
men whereby we must be saved." There is but one
mediator between God and man. *One* name given. *One*
Savior found. *One* sacrifice offered. *One* Gospel
preached. That name and Savior is Jesus. That sacrifice, the blood of Christ, shed on the Cross. That Gospel,
the Gospel of Christ. But *one* door for the profligate
and the moral, for the profane and the professor, for
the publican and the Pharisee, the rich and the poor,
the learned and the illiterate, the aged and the young,
monarch and slave — for *all.* Jesus is THE way. Jesus
is the ONLY way. THE refuge. The ONLY refuge. The
dying thief found it so. Zacchaeus found it so. The
woman at the well in Sychar found it so. *One* door
and the *only* door for the whole wicked world. He is
the way and the door — and whosoever refuseth or re-
jecteth Him must be excluded. But whosoever entereth
in by Christ shall obtain eternal life. He was THE
door from the instant the first promise was announced
in Eden where despair had pitched his pavilions on
man's sterile and blasted estate. He has been the open
door of mercy from that period until now. The way to
God has not been closed a single moment. During the
thousands of years that have rolled onward in their
courses, Jesus Christ has remained fixed in His media-

torial office. Changing never, He is the same yesterday, today and forever. How blessed is the consideration that, whether by day or night, the seeking sinner can never find this door of hope and life closed against him. Jesus will relax the grip of death from every seeking soul. He will unshackle the feet. He will for every prisoner of sin break in the dungeon with the beam of His cross. He will pick from His crown of thorns gems enough to make any seeking sinner's brow have on it the glory of victory. And He *only* is "able, willing, mighty to save." Other refuge have we none. Our helpless souls hang on Him.

But, thinking of Jesus, we consider

IV — The Privilege of the Gospel—
    "If ANY man."

"Any" means "any"— just as "every" means "every"—just as "whosoever" has no other meaning than "whosoever." And "any" includes everybody — everybody of all races and kindreds and tongues and tribes upon the face of the earth. "Him that cometh unto me I will in no wise cast out." Thieves. Murderers. Idolaters. Adulterers — and whosoever loveth and maketh a lie. All who are guilty of the works of the flesh, which are these: adultery, fornication, uncleanness, lasciviousness, idolatry, witchcraft, hatred, variance, emulations, wrath, strife, seditions, heresies, envyings, murders, drunkenness, revelings, and such like (Gal. 5: 19-21).

> "Whosoever heareth," shout, shout the sound!
>   Spread the blessed tidings all the world around;
>   Spread the joyful news wherever man is found:
>   "Whosoever will may come."

"Whosoever will, whosoever will,"
Send the proclamation over vale and hill;
'Tis a loving Father calls the wand'rer home:
"Whosoever will may come."

*And the Spirit and the bride say, Come. And let him
that heareth say, Come. And let him that is athirst
come. And whosoever will, let him take the water
of life freely.*—Rev. 22:17

In the wicked cities of the United States, this is true—
whosoever will may come. In prostrate France and
papal Italy, this is true. In other countries where seas
of martyrs' blood have been shed, many have bowed
in contrition at the Cross — and have found peace.
Yonder "where the juggernauts of India roll" many
have come to have and to hold the peace that passeth
all understanding. Yonder in the Philippines this is
true — there where are smiling and friendly people,
physically freed by Admiral Dewey's guns, intellec-
tually freed by educational missionaries from America,
freed from bondage to relics and friars by the liber-
ating truth of Christ. Whosoever will! Yonder in
Mexico this is true — there where there are dark-faced
people with their quaint courtesies, held back by centuries of illiteracy, chained by age-long superstition,
halted at Guadalupe when they should go on to Calvary — our neighbors in geography, who should be our
closer neighbors in Christ. Whosoever will! Yonder
in Japan this is true. There where the Japanese are
agile seekers for the world's trade and for oriental
rulership — with their shrewd eyes that see everything
and their polite eyes that stare at nothing. Perils
they are if they know the crude and coarse power of
our civilization without knowing our redeeming Christ.
Possibilities of eternal good they are if their attempt at

leadership and dominance comes itself under the leadership of the Lord Jesus Christ who being national is still universal. And yonder they are in China — slaves of a long and drowsy past — their eyes on the tombs of their fathers until such time as the Babe of Bethlehem shall turn their faces to the cradles of their children. Yellow hordes they will be if, like other nations, they are captured by the militaristic devil, but golden throngs they will be if marshaled by the Prince of Peace. Whosoever will! Yonder in India this is true — India with its thirty million gods and dire poverty. Yonder in many lands this is true — lands with hunger and mobs of beggars. Here in our land it is true — with the innumerable miseries that come tramping in from many lands, with its evil "isms" that need to become "wasisms," with its millions of malcontents — whosoever will may come — come to the Christ who has "a balm for every wound and a cordial for every care." You cannot find anybody who has been excluded from God's compassionate words — "God so loved the *world.*"

> *And if any man sin, we have an advocate with the Father, Jesus Christ the righteous: And he is the propitiation for our sins: and not for ours only, but also for the sins of the whole world.*—I JOHN 2: 1-2

The Gospel freely invites all — without respect to country, age or character, to come unto God by Him. There never was, nor is, nor ever will be, any other exclusion than that of the sinner's impenitence and unbelief.

But, looking upon the crucified Christ, we must not overlook

V — THE PARTICULAR OF THE GOSPEL — *"Enter in."*

Entering must be done. The door to a house avails nothing for entrance unless one *enters*. The door is open. But sinners will never enjoy the refuge and the glories of the inside until they enter. To be near is not to be inside. To be almost in but not in is to be altogether outside, even as to be almost saved is to be altogether damned. To be one step outside is to be just as much outside as to be a mile away from the door. Inside the house the fire burns, but you will not feel its cheering warmth until you are inside. Inside the house the feast is spread — and there is plenty for all, but you cannot partake on the outside. Inside, the bed is good for rest, but you can never utilize that bed for rest until you are inside. The men who were, in the days of Joshua, saved from the pursuer had to be inside the cities of refuge, else they would have died. The kindred of Rahab, the harlot, in the days when Jericho fell, had to be inside her house. The folks who were saved in Noah's day, when the wild floods covered the mountains, had to be inside the ark. The sheep, to be safe from the bloodthirsty wolves, had to be *inside* the fold — not near, but in — not almost inside, but altogether inside. To be outside the kingdom is to be outside salvation and refuge — just as to be outside, though near, the lifeboat when the ship goes down is to be at the mercy of the sea. "Thou art *not far* from the kingdom of God" can never be translated to mean "Thou art *in* the kingdom of God."

And now, with thanks unto God for His unspeakable gift, let us give thought to

VI — THE PROMISE OF THE GOSPEL—
"*Shall be saved.*"

And this promise is no unavailing "seppuku." Can a man atone for his own sin by giving his own life? It is a Japanese belief that he can. They use the word "seppuku," meaning "suicidal atonement." Some years ago, when the Graf Zeppelin arrived safely in Los Angeles from Japan, the Chicago Tribune published a copyright dispatch from Tokyo telling what the success of the trip meant to a score of Japanese families. For if the Zeppelin had not crossed the Pacific safely, six officers of the Japanese navy and a dozen or more enlisted men would probably have killed themselves. At the Japanese airport a slight accident had occurred to the Zeppelin. The Japanese commander of the ground crew and several of his officers and men planned suicide, but they desisted when Dr. Eckener made it plain to them that he blamed no one for the accident. However, it came out later that Commander Iraki and a group of officers and men "had solemnly agreed to end their lives if the Graf Zeppelin failed in its Pacific hop." They felt that any failure would be their responsibility because the ship, they believed, would have succeeded if the mishap in Japan had not occurred. All reason for their "seppuku," however, disappeared when the great airship reached Los Angeles. It is a pathetic and tragic mistake that has this death-grip on sincere Japanese men and women. The Tribune called attention to the fact that when thirty-thousand persons were burned to death in the last earthquake, the police captain, lieutenant, and seven patrolmen who had directed them to the fatal field stood before the station house following the tragedy and shot themselves. This, they believed, was "suicidal atonement." Now the newspapers are full of the rumor that Baron Tanaka, former Premier of Japan, caused his own death because of recent political scandals. And all the while, God has revealed that only one death can atone. It must be the death of a sinless man, willing to take the place of sinners and die in their stead. His death atones for all mistakes, all sins, of those who accept His sacrifice. Not "seppuku," but the death of the Son of God, our Savior, is our atonement.

Moreover, praising Christ whom the angels worship, let us rejoice in

VII — The Possessed Provisions of the Gospel.

We find that in the simple and beautiful statement that every believer shall "go in and out and find pasture." Plenteous provision for the believer. Priceless, purchased possessions for the believer. "Plenteous grace with thee is found, grace to cover all my sin." Yes— and plenteous pasture for growth and development also is found—in Christ. No stint. No skimp. No desert. God, as shepherd, leads us in green *pastures* — not over barren wastes where no food is, where no springs of water are.

"Shall go in and out." That means liberty. That is what the Psalmist meant who said: "And I will walk at liberty: for I seek thy precepts" (Ps. 119:45). That is what Jesus meant in the synagogue in Nazareth when, reading from "the book of the prophet Esaias," He said: "The Spirit of the Lord is upon me because he hath sent me . . . to set at liberty them that are bruised" (Luke 4:18). And Paul, writing to the Romans, spoke of "the glorious liberty of the children of God" (Rom. 8:21). So also was Paul's exhortation to the Galatians:

"Stand fast therefore in the liberty wherewith Christ hath made us free, and be not entangled again with the yoke of bondage" (Gal. 5:1). But, along with that, let us remember that he also wrote: "For, Brethren, ye have been called unto liberty; only use not liberty for an occasion to the flesh, but by love serve one another" (Gal. 5:13). So an exhortation like unto that did Peter give: "As free, and not using your liberty for a cloke of maliciousness, but as the servants of God" (I Pet. 2:16).

Jesus—"his own self bare our sins in his own body on the tree." This therefore is the glorious liberty of the Gospel. The sins that are on you and in you are laid on Christ. "God hath laid on him the iniquity of us all." When the burden is placed on Him, you are no more under sin but under grace — the unlimited and unmerited favor of God to the utterly undeserving. You are free — translated from the kingdom of darkness into the kingdom of God's dear Son. "And when the Son shall make you free, you shall be free indeed."

And — think ye! — at what a price our liberty was bought! What a price Jesus paid on the Cross!

United States history records the building of a great transcontinental railway line which would unite the country by rail from Atlantic to Pacific. During construction, financial embarrassment overtook the promoters and with difficulty they secured the funds. There was rejoicing when the work was resumed. The day came when the last rail was to be laid on the border line between New Mexico and Colorado. It was planned to be a great event. A special order was sent to California for a laurel wood tie and two silver spikes were ordered — one for Colorado and one for New Mexico. The Governor of each state was invited. They were to drive the two silver spikes into the laurel wood tie, thus completing the work of construction, making a way of transportation from ocean to ocean and binding together the two states.

As the Governors drove the two silver spikes into the laurel tie the great crowd applauded and a tapped telegraph wire bore the news with a flash, out to the entire country and world! It was a great feat and accomplishment.

There was a day when four spikes were driven, not into a laurel tie, but into the cursed tree and through the hands and feet of the Son of God! They were not spikes of silver, but of iron or steel and driven while Heaven, earth and underearth looked on. When the last spike was driven, a shout went up from all the creation — the news flashed to the ends of the world, for a way of transportation from sin and its darkness had been completed! "It is finished" was the cry! The way was now open from earth to Heaven! There was a trail to the end! A means of access to God has been completed! The spikes were not driven by friends, but by enemies, for it was while we were yet enemies Christ died for us! The last spike driven through the hands of the Son of God on the rugged cross brought man and God together! It was a reconciling death! It was a peace-making transaction! The bonded indebtedness was now fully met and the debt was paid. It was on a certain paschal day in the reign of Tiberius that the bond fell due. The Holy One and the Just One came forward in surety and cried: "Set that to Mine account." He climbed that Cross, that cursed tree, with an unforced will! He yielded His hands to those spikes of iron and from the spike of iron came forth the "rod of iron" with which He will yet rule the nations!

Chapter Six

COLLEGE STUDENTS CONQUERING WITH CHRIST

We are more than conquerors through him who loved us.—Rom. 8:37

Thanks be unto God who giveth us the victory through our Lord Jesus Christ.—I Cor. 15:37

"In all these things — tribulation, distress, persecution, famine, nakedness, peril, sword — we are more than conquerors through him that loved us," says the Apostle Paul who himself, in service to Christ, was "in stripes above measure, in prisons more frequent, in deaths oft" (II Cor. 11:23) — "in perils of waters, in perils of robbers, in perils by his own countrymen, in perils by the heathen, in perils in the city, in perils among false brethren."

"Thanks be unto God who giveth us the victory through our Lord Jesus Christ," he also exultingly exclaims— "he who, enduring hardness as a good soldier of Jesus Christ, was in weariness and painfulness, in watchings often, in hunger and thirst, in fastings often, in cold and nakedness." Not one tone of uncertainty in all this transcendently triumphant language. And certainties are not only the culmination of experiences and discovery, but certainties are starting points. In mathematics we do not argue as to the truth of the statement that a straight line is the shortest distance between two points — that things which are equal to the same thing are equal to each other. In the chemical laboratory we drop mercury into napthalene and with certainty we get phthalic acid. In the foundry we add seven-tenths of one per cent chromium, a corrosion resisting substance, to low carbon steel and thus we surely add forty-five thousand pounds to the tensile strength of low carbon steel. And if we look through the microscope we are sure to see a world in a drop of water. If we look, any clear night, at "the infinite meadows of heaven," through some great telescope, there would be no doubt as to our viewing landscapes fifteen miles away. If we gaze into a properly-adjusted spectograph we, without doubt, learn the constituent elements of the remotest astral bodies — the gold in the sun, the copper on Mars, the iron on the moons of Jupiter. Take a drop of iodine and drop it into a tub full of water — and you know, with absolute certainty, that that drop of iodine colors seven thousand times its weight in water. Stick a burning match into a barrel of gun powder — and you will certainly have an explosion. But with more certainty can you know that in all the matters of life and death, in all the small and great matters that have relation to time and eternity you, even as all men and women everywhere who seek to do the will of God, we can conquer with Christ. And there is no probably, no maybe, no perhaps, no hope-so, no think-so, no uncertainty about it. Rather — absolute certainty.

I would put, with tenderness and yet with the noticeableness of a sharp sword point, some questions against your very heart — and then answer those questions. The first question is—

I — Who Conquers ?

The answer is: "We." "*We* are more than conquerors"— conquerors plus. "Who giveth *us* the victory." So *we* are the victors. *We* — with bodies with which we are so mysteriously bound up, bodies "fearfully and wonderfully made," bodies dull and tuneless in themselves but which may be harps on which the music of piety is struck to heaven. *We*— with brains with their different departments and compartments and functions. *We* — with the memory, the irresistible conviction of personal identity with the past. *We* — with the personality force as perplexing as electricity, as actual and baffling as gravitation, as potent and indefinable as heat. *We* — with individual responsibility which can never honorably bear the brand of "transferable." *We*—with our youth that hastens so swiftly to old age. *We* — with our sorrows and joys. *We* — with our weaknesses, with our loves, with our dislikes. *We* — with friends and enemies. *We* — with our hungers and satisfactions. *We* — with heartaches, with sins, with prayers, with perversities. *We* — with our faults and follies, with our social and individual duties inevitably blended. *We* — with our befuddlements and befoulments. *We* — knowing the sordid tricks the world inevitably plays upon all souls that yield to its horrible charms. *We* — knowing how the world "lures with the spangles of its false wealth and then crushes within the waiting folds of its merciless power." *We* — with the pungent power of high decision, with the hunger that longs for the fulness of life, with the visions that flash down from the shining peaks of the ideal. *We* — related to the *past* in the matter of those who have handed down to us blood-bought legacies. *We* — related to the *present* in the matter of how we are to live and meet the demands and challenges of a day in which spiritual mercury falls low. *We* — in a strange day when faith's wings are clipped by reason's scissors, when black snow falls, when the fury of life's fierce heat burns divine dew off the grass, — a day when civilization is called a "conglomerate huddle of unrelatedness"— a day when we hear people say, as Victor Hugo said:

> But in this boasted march of wrong and error,
> 'Mid the vast splendor of an age that glows,
> One thing, O Jesus, fills my heart with terror—
> The echo of Thy voice still feebler grows.

We — related to the future in the matter of what we shall hand down to posterity to testify that we were heroes and not "dumb driven cattle" in the battles. *We* — related to eternity with its Judgment — because of the unquestioned fact of immortality. *I* can conquer. *You* can conquer. *We* can conquer — with Christ, who challenges us to make the venture into the realms of abiding reality, who would have us know assuredly that "Christianity is the intersphering of the finite with the infinite," who would have us to burn pure at the interior of our being and meet life's perilous situations with indomitable bravery and "whip death to death one thousand times"—turning blight into bloom, turning gloom into light, believing that real happiness is not mostly pleasure but mostly victory, believing that happiness often has difficulty for its setting and adventure for its strength. For—

> Real glory
> Springs from the silent conquest of ourselves,
> And without that the conqueror is naught,
> But the first slave.

God would have us to maintain an uncompromising enmity toward the false, an invincible friendship toward the true.

This brings us to the second question — and some answers.

II — Where Can We Conquer ?

In what realms can we conquer with Christ? In what fields — with their wheat and their tares? In what forests — with inviting strong oaks and repulsive thorn trees? In what gardens — with their roses and their brambles? In what realms — with their storms and calms? On what roads — with their stretches and turns, open spaces and dark tunnels? On what seas— with their silences and their simoons? In what seasons— with their sunshine and clouds, with their flowers and their frosts, with their warmth and wintry cold? Well, we may have affliction, persecution, anguish, privation, peril, and, maybe, the beheading sword. But these will not confuse us or stagger us into despair or defeat. Nothing in the known or the unknown, nothing in the present or the future, nothing human or inhuman, nothing that will or can happen shall snap asunder "the adamantine bond that binds us and God together in victorious conquest." Conquer we shall in the delightful elements of life — where we see many gay butterflies, where we watch fluttering doves, where we hear silver-throated nightingales. Conquer we shall in the painful things of life — where we deal with vicious hawks, sword-mouthed sharks, crocodiles, mad dogs, rattlesnakes and microbes. Conquer we shall—enabled by His grace and guidance to sing the song of "The Husbandman":

> I break the soil with anguished pain,
>   And sow with bitter tears.
> My soul doth reap like golden grain
>   The gladness of the year.
>
> I hear the winds that roar and roar,
>   The elements that rush.
> My soul doth hear evermore
>   The high celestial hush!
>
> I *win* in darkness black as death
>   The scant bread of the sod,
> My soul doth bring from fields of faith
>   The living sheaves of God.

Where can we conquer? *In the realm of the physical.*
The body, our constant companion, is the basis of all
man's manifold activities. Many, victims of the errors
of monasticism, have ignored the body, giving attention only to the soul. Many, looking upon the body as
essentially evil, have set all the militant energies of
their personality in battle array against its assertion of
supremacy. Many, allowing the spirit to abdicate and
the body to sit on the throne, have surrendered to
the body.

So we have the rigid austerity of the ascetic. So we
have the indulgence of the voluptuary. So we have the
works of the flesh which are "adultery, fornication, uncleanness, lasciviousness, idolatry, witchcraft, hatred,
variance, emulations, wrath, strife, seditions, heresies,
envyings, murders, drunkenness, revelings and such
like." So we have the sowing to the flesh and the corrupt reaping thereof. So we have the hereditary channel befouled with unclean blood. Thus men cheat themselves and burglarize their own lives and dishonor God
by failure to present to God their bodies, "a living
sacrifice, holy, acceptable unto God." Thus men fool-

ishly refuse to let sin reign in the mortal body. Thus, with many wrong conceptions of what it means to glorify God in the body, many are not "always bearing about in the body the dying of the Lord Jesus that the life also of Jesus might be made manifest in the mortal flesh." Thus, looking on the body as essentially evil, many are forgetting that "we who die are always delivered unto death for Jesus' sake that the life also of Jesus might be made manifest in our mortal body."

We need to conquer in the realm of the physical. Then do we pass from the feverishness of living into the more blessed experience of *life*. But to conquer in this realm is not play work, but battle work. Some conception of the constancy and strain of the battle for victory in the physical realm Carlyle gives in these words:

> Seated within this body's car,
> The silent self is driven far,
> And the five senses at the poles,
> Like steeds are tugging restive of control.
>
> And if the driver lose his way
> Or the reins break, who can say
> Into what blind paths, what pits of fear
> Will plunge the chargers in their mad career?

And it is no little battle that must be waged before all the members of the body are made servants of a loving will, the representatives of kindly thoughts, the ambassadors of a great heart — instruments of righteousness in the service of our Lord Jesus.

And the tragedy of defeat when the body is permitted to be the foe of the invisible splendors of spiritual realities is set forth by Mrs. Wilcox, who writes:

> God gave him passions splendid as the sun,
> Meant for the lordliest purposes—a part
> Of Nature's full and fertile mother's heart,
> From which new systems and new worlds are spun.
> And now behold! Behold what he has done!
> In Folly's court and Carnal Pleasure's mart
> He flung the wealth God gave him at the start.
> At dawn he stood potential, opulent.
> With virile manhood and emotions keen.
> At noon he stands—all Love's large fortune spent
> In petty traffic, unproductive, mean—
> A pauper cursed with impotent desire.

And the certainty of victory in conquering in the realm of the physical, Paul expressed in these words: "But I keep my body under, and bring it into subjection, lest that by any means, when I have preached to others, I myself should become a castaway."

And the same strenuous conflict issuing in victory, Tennyson expressed. As a younger poet he wrote:

> Oh, for a man to arise in me
> That the man I am may cease to be.

But as an older man, after many roses had withered under many frosts and snows, he said:

> I gaze upon the fields of the past,
> Where I sank with the body at times,
> In the slough of low desire;
> But now I have no yelp of the heart,
> And the man is quiet at last;
> As I stand upon the heights
> With a glimpse of a height that is higher.

Again we ask: *"Where can we conquer?"* In the realm of *thought*. In many places Paul, Aristotle and Demosthenes of the Jewish race, apostle who left a trail of glory across the Gentile world, gives us the secret of possessing interior spiritual richness. And that secret is his urge to us to keep thinking, thinking, thinking on the high and noble—not slipshod thinking, not "intellectual crazy quilt weaving." But let him say it: "Finally, brethren, whatsoever things are true, whatsoever things are honest, whatsoever things are just, whatsoever things are pure, whatsoever things are lovely, whatsoever things are of good report; if there be any virtue, and if there be any praise, think on these things" (Phil. 4:8).

In accepting this and looking upon this urge as a commandment — in so thinking — we are wiser than when we accept the physicist's truth about corpuscles, the astronomer's truth about the movements of the satellites of Uranus and Neptune, the mathematician's truth about numbers, the painter's truth about colors, the poet's truth about rhythmic verbal combinations, the pharmacist's truth about medicines. For thought is a wonderful power.

By means of thought you can travel to the uttermost parts in time and space. By means of thought you hear the eloquence of world-famed orators, ponder the wisdom of the greatest philosophers, recount the glory of ancient nations, sit at the feet of Socrates and Dante and Shakespeare and Milton and Jesus, and let them speak.

By means of thought we march with Caesar's armies, join Napoleon's campaigns, sit in the councils of the world, paint with Raphael, stand with Angelo as from "the sterile womb of stone he raises children with God," stand near Beethoven as he "makes surging seas of tone subservient to his rod."

By means of thought, we can travel beyond the dim centuries and see the banners float above armed hosts and conquerors riding to victories that have changed the course of time. By means of thought, we can go with Columbus as he touches the shores of a new world, with Magellan as he circles the globe, with Hugh Miller among the rocks, with Galileo among the gardens of the stars, with Faraday along the roadways of molecules and atoms. By means of thought, we can journey on pathless oceans and listen to the voices of forgotten seers, to dead poets singing to us the deeds of mighty men and the love of beautiful women. By means of thought, we can listen to the war horns of King Olaf wail across the floods, to harps sounding high festival in forgotten halls, to the thunder of war guns, to the songs and shouts of men who, choosing the garments of flame and blood for their garments of glory, walked across the shuddering earth and gave their lives to make secure the imperiled liberties of the world. By means of thought we can sit down with the kings of Nineveh as they drink from cups of ivory and gold. By means of thought we can enter at leisure into the intellectual heritage of the centuries. By means of thought we can view the kingdoms of the world, their cradles and tombs, their glory and their tragedy.

A poet has pictured a dweller in a drab village answering the question: "How can you live in Goshen— a wretched little place, where people talk about tawdry things and plant cabbages in the moonlight?" And the answer was: "But I do not live in Goshen, but in Greece where Plato taught and Phidias carved — in Rome, where Cicero penned immortal lines and Michael Angelo dreamed things of beauty."

Mind is as a ship at sea—and it needs a pilot. For this sea of life has shallows of speculation, treacherous shoals of false philosophies, storms of doubt, typhoons of tribulation, waterspouts of cynicism, whirlpools of agnostic surmises, currents of atheistic denials, tidal waves of foolish conceits. But with Christ as Pilot, furnishing chart and compass, we, conquering in the realm of thought, shall surely possess the wealth of wisdom which is from above, which, as the divinely inspired writer puts it, "is first pure, then peaceable, gentle, easy to be entreated, full of mercy and good fruits, without variance and without hypocrisy."

When Heine's friend inquired after his health, the poet replied: "I feel a little stupid, rather dull." "I am sorry," said the inquirer, "what's the matter?" "I've just been exchanging thoughts with Dumas." There was Heine's statement that dull thoughts produce mental stupidity. But we have the evidence, often in what we hear, often in what we read, often in conversations, that godless thoughts produce spiritual aridity. For there is much dull and wrong thinking in the world today — and many counterfeit coins of thought in circulation. There are many mental jaybirds squawking raucously — labeling their chatter wisdom. Many mental owls there are moaning and hooting from philosophical cypress trees — giving men the chill of despondency rather than the warmth of cheer and encouragement. Many mental squirrels there are quarreling noisily over nonessentials, preferring to fuss over the frills than to praise the garments of humility and truth. Many wild mental eagles there are flapping well-plumed wings and screaming wildly — while their sharp talons tear at our reliable franchise of Christian hopes. Some mental butcher birds there are also whose pens are mercilessly deadly rapiers. Yes, there is a lot of so-called advanced thought which is a fine name for some very abominable principles. Then, too, in this varied life of ours "quivering with unexpectedness, swift with breaking wonder, veiled with unplucked mysteries, trembling with silent horrors," there are some mental vultures who feast on carrion — and would have us feed on the same.

We shudder to think of the mental powers exerted today in repudiating the authority of God and Christ in morals — boldly rejecting the sanctity of the home and the ethics and idealism of marriage in the interest of behaviourism and self-expression—sneering at the foundations of Christian conduct. There is the easy-going mental exertion — whatever is is right. There is the narrow and selfish mental product of utilitarianism — whatever seems best for the majority is right. There is the variable mental conception of custom— whatever happens to be common anywhere is right. There is the gone-mad mental conception of individualism — whatever comes to me as right is right. There is that desperate mental extreme where anarchy and despotism meet — nothing is right and everything is wrong and might is right. There is that selfish tendency in thought.

Such knowledge makes us say what one other has said:

> I hate your mind.
> It is a sharp-pointed sword,
> Forged of well-tempered steel,
> Which stabs and cuts, but never bends,
> Aimed unerringly for a victim's heart,
> But never damaged by the blood it draws.
>
> I hate your mind.
> Like a high-powered locomotive,
> Swift-moving over exactly parallel rails
> To a desired end, it unfallibly arrives,
> But without seeing blossom or tree,
> Never knowing if a body lies crushed beneath it.

May we so conquer in the realm of thought that nobody can hear what we speak, read what we write, know what we do, know what we are, know what we think — and say: "I hate your mind."

It was said of Ingersoll: "Blest with a magnificent presence — a voice almost matchless in its richness, range and beauty, and in the power of superb eloquence, yet, because of unconsecrated mental powers, because of much crooked thinking, he prostituted that divine gift to such base uses as the exaltation of atheistic agnosticism, scorn of the Holy Scriptures, and the overthrow of the faith of believers in Jesus. His mental powers were as a jewel of gold in a swine snout!"

But it was said of Gladstone: "In Christ his impetuous temper found restraint, in Christ his versatile personality found fulfillment, in Christ *his mighty intellect* found anchorage."

With Christ let us go forth conquering and to conquer in the realm of thought—knowing that God "understands our thoughts afar off." With Christ let us make our world big and not little, clean and not dirty—never letting our thoughts be thoughts of iniquity. With Christ, let us conquer doubts and fears—never letting it be said of us: "Their thoughts accusing or excusing one another are evil." With Christ, let us conquer in the realm of thought, giving not one minute of hospitality to infidelic thought so that it will never be known of us on earth or recorded of us in heaven: "God is not in all their thoughts."

Jesus, who exalted character above reputation, religion above ritual, substance above form, reality above appearance, opens the door of high thought and mental achievements to us. From the intellectual conceit unaware of the rattle of dry bones, from the superficial mental illumination that lacks the urge of sacrificial passion, from the tragedy of contracting spiritual boundaries while extending intellectual frontiers, he delivers. He makes it so that no matter what man and circumstances do to you outwardly, they cannot prevent you from living inwardly in the companionship of high thoughts. He opens the doors which nobody can shut.

The Roman Empire could put narrow limitations around John's body, but it could put no narrow limitations around John's mind. Marooned on Patmos, he saw a new heaven and a new earth wherein dwelleth righteousness. Through Christ, Paul, in prison, could say, "Whatsoever things are true, honest, just, pure, lovely, of good report—*think* on these things!" In prison, John Bunyan's mind roved the earth and heaven. And he wrote a book that escaped the jail, traveled more highways and walked more bypaths and knocked at more doors and spoke to more people in their mother tongue than any book save the Bible.

Suffice it to say that in the mental realm we can make ours the experience of Paul who wrote:

> *Casting down imaginations, and every high thing that exalteth itself against the knowledge of God, and bringeth into captivity every thought to the obedience of Christ.*—II Cor. 10:5

Let us ask once more: *Where* can we conquer? In the realm of temptation—no matter where the temptation arises, no matter how subtle and strong the temptation is. And how that truth strengthens and sustains "as we go toward the sunrising of heaven's perfect day."

Scientists say that blood flows more freely to the

sound of music. And surely our blood will flow more courageously when we read from the Bible, book above and beyond all books as an ocean is beyond a tub in glory and wisdom, these precious words:

There hath no temptation taken you but such as is common to man: but God is faithful, who will not suffer you to be tempted above that ye are able; but will with the temptation also make a way to escape, that ye may be able to bear it.—I COR. 10:13

For in that he himself hath suffered being tempted, he is able to succour them that are tempted.
—HEB. 2:18

For we have not an high priest which cannot be touched with the feeling of our infirmities; but was in all points tempted like as we are, yet without sin. Let us therefore come boldly unto the throne of grace, that we may obtain mercy, and find grace to help in time of need.—HEB. 4: 15-16

How we rejoice in this when we know that an unconquered temptation means certain disaster sometime—somewhere.

But with Christ, who conquered the world, man's external enemy — conquered the flesh, man's internal enemy — conquered Satan, man's infernal enemy — we, yielding to Christ and following Christ, will find all the spears that Satan, the enemy of our souls, thrusts at us as brittle as macaroni sticks. We will find all the fires he kindles for our burning as feeble and as enduring as candles in hurricanic winds. We shall learn that "none of the weapons formed against us shall prosper."

> Yield not to temptation,
>   For yielding is sin;
> Each vict'ry will help you
>   Some other to win;

Fight manfully onward,
    Dark passions subdue;
Look ever to Jesus,
    He'll carry you through.

Ask the Savior to help you,
    Comfort, strengthen, and keep you;
He is willing to aid you,
    He will carry you through.

Surely the promises which Christ made to the churches mentioned in the Revelation we can appropriate as our very own — precious promises that never fail of fulfillment:

To him that overcometh will I give to eat of the tree of life, which is in the midst of the paradise of God.
—Rev. 2:7

He that overcometh shall not be hurt of the second death.—Rev. 2:11

To him that overcometh will I give to eat of the hidden manna, and will give him a white stone, and in the stone a new name written, which no man knoweth saving he that receiveth it.—Rev. 2:17

And he that overcometh, and keepeth my works unto the end, to him will I give power over the nations.
—Rev. 2:26

He that overcometh, the same shall be clothed in white raiment; and I will not blot out his name out of the book of life, but I will confess his name before my Father, and before his angels.—Rev. 3:5

Him that overcometh will I make a pillar in the temple of my God, and he shall go no more out: and I will write upon him the name of my God, and the name of the city of my God, which is new Jerusalem, which cometh down out of heaven from my God: and I will write upon him my new name.—Rev. 3:12

Now we ask: WHERE can we conquer — with Christ? In the realm of death. How stark a fact is death! And how often, even more than we are willing to acknowledge, do many of us think upon death — death whose only palace is a huge skull, whose only gold is the dust of the grave, whose only pleasure fountains are the falling tears of the world. Somewhere I read this poem—by Devito:

> When you're a child, Death seems to be a place
> Like Paris, California, or Palm Beach,
> Or any other nice place out of reach,
> Where people stay till you forget their face.
>
> Then you are grown and Death is like a hawk,
> A vicious bird of prey circling above,
> Waiting to carry off the ones you love
> And eat them in his aerie on a rock.
>
> When you are old, you suddenly are wise,
> And know Life as the monstrous bird of prey,
> Eating men's hearts and plucking out their eyes,
> Or destroying them some other, subtler way—
> Then you see Death, a kind hand everywhere,
> Snapping off lights that are too bright to bear.

Let us not forget, dread death as we may, and as many do, that there is a time coming when death, the one mocker at all our hopes and joys, the impish satirist who laughs and leers when our hearts ache, shall be swallowed up in victory.

> *So when this corruptible shall have put on incorruption, and this mortal shall have put on immortality, then shall be brought to pass the saying that is written, Death is swallowed up in victory. O death, where is thy sting? O grave, where is thy victory? The sting of death is sin; and the strength of sin is the law. But thanks be to God, which giveth us the victory through our Lord Jesus Christ.*
>
> —I Cor. 15: 54-57

Once I was out hunting in the woods with my young son — when the sun seemed to drop out of sight, as a cloud arose, and darkness came upon us and the winds blew and some night birds wildly and weirdly called. Afraid, my little son said: "Dad, have you been here before?" "Yes," I answered calmly. "And do you know the way out of here so we can get in the road home?" "Yes, I know the way out," I said. His grateful sigh of relief was as one who has suddenly had a burden lifted.

Now we journey, if we be not among those who are alive when Jesus returns again to earth, to the land of death. In that land, we are told, there is darkness and silence and coldness and aloneness. But Jesus has been in that land — in it and through it. He knows all about it. He knows "the way out to the road home." And He says to us: "Fear not, it is dark in there, but I am the light of the world, and he that followeth me shall not walk in darkness, but shall have the light of life. It is cold in there, but close to my heart, where I'll hold you, it is warm. I know all about the darkness. I know all about the silence and the coldness and the aloneness. But I conquered it. And so shall *you*. And *you*. And all who believe in me — and follow where I lead." "I am persuaded that . . . death . . . can not separate us from the love of God which is in Christ Jesus, our Lord."

Kingsley asked: "Death, beautiful, wise, kind Death, when will you come and tell me what I want to know?" And not long before his passing, his daughter heard him, unconscious of any human presence, say aloud: "How beautiful is God!"

A devoted Christian mother, coming to the passing hour, said to her loved ones: "Children, going through the valley of shadows is like cutting a path through the grass and flowers. I see a white city on a silver ocean."

> A lone thrush sings as the night begins,
> A rich, wild song as the darkness falls;
> And a secret peace sweeps over the world—
> Over the starry halls!
> So may I sing on the edge of death,
> When the dark descends and the hours depart;
> So may the mystic peace drop down
> Over my tired heart.

III — With Whom Can We Conquer?

"We are more than conquerors *through* him who *loved* us." "Thanks be unto God who giveth us the victory *through our Lord Jesus Christ.*" "Christ is the way; men without him are Cains, wanderers, vagabonds. Christ is the truth; without him men are liars like the devil of old. Christ is the life; without him men are dead in trespasses and sin. Christ is the light; without him men are in darkness and go they know not whither. Christ is the vine; without him men are withered branches prepared for the fire. Christ is the Rock; without him men are carried away with the flood."

The Apostle had it right when he said: "Christ in you the hope of glory!" Not the glory of the future, but the glory of character and victorious conquest here and now, the glory of success after failure, the glory of a well-rounded and developed womanhood and manhood with Christ enunciating Himself through the precincts of personality! Jesus will prompt us in our perplexities, help us in our hazards, direct us in our doubts, guide us in our glooms. In Him and by Him we "mount up with wings as eagles"; by Him we find the "mountains brought low, the valleys exalted, the crooked places made straight, the rough places plain."

For He is our Lord — so mightily alive. Alive, linking the exploits of the fathers to the achievements of the children. Alive, giving us, amid the snarling clamors of the day, voices that will not die away in error and incompetence. Alive, offering the inexhaustible fountains of His strength. Alive, to the end of unending eternity — acknowledging no mastery in hostile circumstances. Alive, keeping pace with the most unexpected challenges. Alive, able, willing, mighty to help — our eternal contemporary. A living Christ will give us VICTORY.

He gave victory to the courageous saints of the early church, leading them on to the most sublime adventures of human history. He, "conquering Rome more completely than did Hannibal or Attila, made of the heathen coliseum a Christian church, set up a spiritual empire by the Golden Horn more extensive and potent than the temporal throne of Constantine."

> Conquering now and still to conquer,
>   Rideth a King in His might,
> Leading the host of all the faithful
>   Into the midst of the fight;
> See them with courage advancing,
>   Clad in their brilliant array,
> Shouting the name of their Leader,
>   Hear them exultingly say:
>
> "Not to the strong is the battle,
>   Not to the swift is the race,
> Yet to the true and the faithful
>   Victory is promised through grace."

Delivered at the
Baptist Student Union State Convention
Columbus, Mississippi
October, 1940

CHAPTER SEVEN

FADING WORDS

Thou hatest instruction, and casteth my words behind thee.—Ps. 50:7

They rebelled against the words of God—Ps. 107: 11

Mine enemies have forgotten thy words.—Ps. 119: 39

EDWARD BOK, great American journalist, met, when Bok was a lad, Ralph Waldo Emerson, when Mr. Emerson was groping in the mental fog that overshadowed his decaying mental faculties — when his mental bow was limp, his quiver emptied. He asked Mr. Emerson to write his own name. Mr. Emerson asked Bok to write it out and he would try to copy it. In trying to copy it, Emerson wrote only the R in Ralph and misspelled Concord. Later, one sad day, Emerson attended Longfellow's funeral. Emerson's mind, like some great cathedral gone to ruins, was still shrouded in mist. Standing at the casket, he looked upon the face of Longfellow, his intimate friend. Shaking his head slowly, with a puzzled frown clouding his brow, he said: "This was a lovely soul, but I *forget* his name."

But a tragedy, one thousand fold sadder, one thousand fold more filled with gloom and ghostly winds that cry and wail, is the country-wide tragedy of fading and forgotten words — a tragedy that, like the tightening

133

arms of an octopus, encircles our nation. There are fading and forgotten words in individual vocabularies, in church vocabularies, in home vocabularies, in business vocabularies, in school vocabularies, in friendship vocabularies, in scientific and theological vocabularies, in preaching vocabularies. Recently, I read some books of sermons by a well-known preacher and not once was the blood of Christ mentioned. Must we give heed to one who, in preaching mentions everything about the fire, but the heat thereof, everything about the rose, but the fragrance thereof, everything about the mind but the thought thereof, everything about music but the melody thereof, everything about the rainbow but the color thereof, everything about the mockingbird, the Beethoven of the boughs, the Mendelssohn of the magnolias, but the singing thereof?

With the hope that I shall, by rebuke,— reproof with attendant longsuffering—and by wooing, re-enthrone in the lives of some of you some forgotten words, I speak of words that have fallen on "sere and yellow days"— words that are with us with the wreckage of "the worm and the canker"— words as hard to find real and dominant in some lives and practices as a needle in a haystack, as a calmness in a cyclone — words that seem to have in some lives only the permanence of a feather in a bonfire — words that have melted away in some lives and churches and homes and communities and nations as ice under the attack of desert suns. Words that seem to function in our lives as sparrows' wings on eagle bodies, as glow worms in midnight, as candles flickering feebly in a hurricane. There are worthy words no longer brought to the front — the words of God which we have discarded as old shoes worn through, as old clothes moth-eaten, as cups of cream filled with flies, as a frock coat so worn that it heliographs in the sun if worn down the street. When the average man's vocabulary is so thin that it flashes its thinness, we wince when certain oft-repeated words, with never-failing weariness, invade the newspaper columns and the pulpit and the schoolroom. Likewise we grieve, as we wait for the use of certain great words, to find them well-nigh forgotten.

A columnist — be that columnist man or woman, I do not know — over ten years ago — speaking on forgotten words, said this: "One diversion which helped us to forget how much money we'd lost in 1931 was the pastime of selecting the ten most beautiful words in the English language. That was easy — because you had only to select a Latin derivative — and there you were! Glamourous, glorious, melodious, luminous, dalliance, romance, caress, ardor, lullaby, murmurous— just like that!

"But, try to think of the ten ugliest words, and immediately you go Anglo-Saxon or fall into American slang. Try these on your singing voice — wretch, snooty, hog, swag, grouch, goggles, lousy, blab, goulash, nob, spinach! And I can think of lots, even more painful to a poet's ear!"

Yet, 'tis not of the loveliest words, nor of the longest words, nor of the ugliest words, but of *forgotten* words we speak now.

But — let me ask — what are some of the good old-fashioned words — words born in the fear of God— words reared in the love of God — words far-reaching in blessed ministry — words clothed in vigorous realities — words that need to be brought to the front again — words to take out of the unemployed ranks and put to work, full time and overtime, again — if our

nation is to endure, our churches to prosper, our homes
to be bulwarked, our lives to be diademed? I mention
a few:

I — OBEDIENCE

1. *Obedience,* not in the dictionary only, but in our
life vocabulary, experienced and manifested in our
lives, has the unspeakable promise of God's blessing.

> *And in thy seed shall all the nations of the earth be
> blessed; because thou hast obeyed my voice.*
> —GEN. 22:18

> *Ye have seen what I did unto the Egyptians, and how
> I bare you on eagles' wings, and brought you unto
> myself. Now therefore, if ye will obey my voice in-
> deed, and keep my covenant, then ye shall be a
> peculiar treasure unto me above all people: for all
> the earth is mine.*—EXOD. 19: 4-5
> *A blessing, if ye obey the commandments of the Lord
> your God, which I command you this day.*
> —DEUT. 11: 27

2. *Obedience is better than sacrifice.* Just one verse
or so from the Bible—book above and beyond all books
as a locomotive is beyond a push cart in carrying
power, will suffice here.

> *And Samuel said, Hath the Lord as great delight in
> burnt offerings and sacrifices, as in obeying the voice
> of the Lord? Behold, to obey is better than sacrifice,
> and to hearken than the fat of rams. For rebellion is
> as the sin of witchcraft, and stubbornness is as in-
> iquity and idolatry.*—I SAM. 15: 22-23

3. *Obedience to God is better than obedience to men.*
Just one chord from the thousand-string harp will fill
a lifetime with music:

> *Then Peter and the other apostles answered and said,
> we ought to obey God rather than men.*—ACTS. 5: 29

The first law God gave man was the law of obedience. No principle is more noble than that of a true obedience. Obedience to truth known is the King's highway to that which is still beyond us. Doing the will of God leaves no time for disputing about His plans. Thirty years of Jesus' wonderful life are hidden in these words: "And he went down with them, and came to Nazareth, and was subject unto them." Dr. Alldredge, statistical secretary, in Southern Baptist Handbook of recent date, states: "Fifty years ago the United States was the most law-abiding nation in the world. Now it is the most lawless. In the past ten years, population has increased seventeen percent in the United States, and crime has increased one hundred and seventeen percent." Obedience an unknown word — save in the dictionary.

And we are not sufficiently repentant to quit our disobedience. Is it the law of decent respect for age and authority? We wave it aside with a smile or a sneer. Is it the law for protection of private property? We form great corporations and give them the determining of prices and often the rights of others. Is it the law for controlling the speed of vehicles? We allow motors to be built with speed four times greater than safety permits. And we left forty thousand dead on our streets and highways last year. Murder by motor. Memories of graves because of it. Is it a prohibition law to abolish the evil of drink? By false claims and political and personal trickery we abolish it. We have dressed up the old liquor hobos—the saloons, who used to live in ragged clothes in the back alleys and put on them a "Prince Albert" suit and patent leather shoes and placed them in drug stores and grocery stores and "liquitoriums" on prominent corners — never seeming to know that we cannot take the odor from the skunk by putting it in a perfume factory, that we cannot take the poison from a rattlesnake by putting it in a decorated neon-lighted room, that we cannot make the porcupine's bristles soft as fur by dressing it in silk. When will we ever have sense enough and concern enough as to our blood-bequeathed legacies to understand that a nation that does not hold her laws sacred will soon—yea, even sooner than we think—have nothing sacred for which to live, nothing priceless for which to fight, nothing valuable for which to suffer? Lincoln said: "Let reverence for law be breathed by every American mother to the lisping babe, let it be taught in the schools, seminaries, colleges; let it be written in primers, spelling books, almanacs; let it be preached from pulpits, proclaimed in the legislative halls, and enforced in the courts of justice; let it become the political religion of the nation."

May it be said of us that in thought, in attitude, in word, in deed we have not forgotten the word itself nor the meaning thereof — obedience. May it be said of us that, preferring the duty we owe to God to any danger that may come from man, we obey the Lord, our God. Then shall our spiritual health and spiritual joy be not a bubble, but a reality — not as a desert tree scorched and fruitless under the breath of the simoon, but as a tree, full-boughed, full-leafed, full-fruited, planted by rivers of water. Then shall we, obeying God rather than men, giving our ears to His commands rather than to the opinions of men, be not like flowers under the blight of the frost, but like flowers under the kiss of the sun. Then shall we avoid the tragedy that is found in Cardinal Woolsey's words, when, thrown aside like a sucked orange upon a rubbish heap, he said: "Had I served God with but half the zeal I have served my King, He would not have left me naked in mine old age to mine enemies."

Another little-known and forgotten word in many individual and national vocabularies is the word

II — Honesty

The notes I myself have endorsed in good faith and have had to pay — after elaborate promises from those who asked me to endorse said notes — squelch any arguments to the contrary. The hundreds of small loans I have made (a few of them to preachers) over a period of thirty years and the very few that have been repaid, make me to wonder if many people ever heard of the word honesty. One man said: "If you'll lend me five dollars, I hope God will turn me black as a negro if I don't pay you in four weeks." That was twenty years ago. Well, maybe God did turn him into a black man — and, through the "nigger" eyes he cannot see the trail to my office door. Another man said: "Help me this one time — and I'll pay you with compound interest, or I hope I'll become a jackass!" Pleadingly, tearfully, he said it. I helped him. And maybe that was he I heard braying ten years later when I was riding by a neighbor's barn.

Honesty is a quaint old word much needed to be brought back and to the forefront today. Many of the young generation seldom hear the word mentioned outside of school. And it is not mentioned then to show that a man is just as much a thief who steals a nickle as one who steals a dollar — just as much a thief who beats the street car company out of a ride — as the burglar who prys open a window and prowls around the house and steals jewelry. And it is mentioned rather lightly then — as a careless physician who puts a measles sign up where smallpox is. Many people today have to look up the word in a dictionary to know what it means. Many people have confused the word "honesty" with "prestige" — forgetting that some folks, when it comes to prestige, are as to honesty internally putrid. Many people have confused "honesty" with "distinction" — not believing that some folks with distinction are extinct in honesty. Many people have "honesty" confused with "ostentation"— not seeming to know that many "showy" folks do not show up well in matters that demand honesty. Many people have "honesty" confused with "popularity"— not understanding that the wolf who robs the sheepfold is popular with wolves, but not with sheep — or shepherds. Some people still think, as one has wisely said, that it's more "honor" to be taken up by the smart crowd than to stand well with their creditors. Or more "honor" to "make" an exclusive club than to make good on a debt or a job or a promise to a friend. Lots of people, despite all they have read and heard about an honest man being "the noblest work of God," still think it quite "honorable" to get money in any way you can— without going to jail.

Stock-gambling shows that honesty needs to be brought back. Racketeering and easy money show that honesty should be given *first* place rather than *no* place. High pressure salesmanship that would, with a benevolent smile that would bless, let you in on the ground floor when there is no ground and no floor, testifies strikingly that honesty should be taken from the footstool and put on the throne. Salesmanship of worthless stocks that have promise of dividends only in the lying mouth of the salesman makes us know that honesty is dressed up in the thinking of some in dunce cap rather than with coronet. Get-rich-quick schemes, which have no more pegs to hang honest hopes upon than the aurora borealis race that "flits ere you can point the place," make us know how dishonesty stalks abroad under the garrulous guise of "I-would-do-you-good, my dear woman." Debt dodging, when there should be debt paying, shows how dishonesty walks with colossal strides, with heavy boots, with libelizing hands, with ungrateful hearts. I know a young man who went broke and lost his home with fifteen thousand dollars owed to him by folks who, over a period of five years, had bought groceries on a credit and, after the eating, put nothing in the hand of him who had put his groceries in their mouths and stomachs. Trade trickery, evasions by bankruptcy, mathematics strangely at variance with honesty in vote counting, government by slickery and trickery — in communities, in cities, in states, in nations — show us the need for a return to the great principle set forth by Henry Clay when he said, "I'd rather be right than President." Too often men say now, "I'd rather be elected — no matter how— than be right." Think of the doctor's bills that are delayed "until a more convenient season," or dodged forever. I know a man, father of seven children, who, though he could have paid, did not pay the doctor for the delivery of his first child until the fourth child was born. Think of the church pledges which people make and which, with the passing of Sunday after Sunday, mean little — and are passed by with a sigh or a sniff or a sneer or an indifferent smile! Think of the bankers and building-and-loan leaders who gamble with or speculatingly invest the money entrusted to them by widows, by orphans, by the aged.

Lots of people are content to get money at the cost of what money cannot buy — honor, friends, happiness, good conscience, surrendered principle. There is dishonesty everywhere: dishonesty at the dairy where a man digs a well to increase his milk supply, instead of buying more cows; dishonesty of employees who get a day's pay and do not give a day's work; dishonesty of employers who receive a day's work and will not give a day's pay; dishonesty at the coal yard where the driver is weighed with the coal; dishonesty at the store where goods of poor quality are put off by slick-tongued saleswomen who tell you anything is "so sweet" on you; dishonesty on the farm where the farmer's bushel is less than standard; dishonesty by buyers who eat groceries from the merchant never intending to pay; dishonesty by readers who refuse to pay subscriptions for papers, cotton sellers who sell themselves with the load, money lenders lending money at 20 percent or more, preacher cheaters who ride away with his money in a host of tears and hard luck lies, politicians with graft and greed, inside and outside, that fester like a carbuncle on the body politic.

Government dishonesties — where men steal elections. Denominational dishonesties — where men become Carnesque. Any Southern Baptist should be able to tell you the meaning of that word. Income tax dishonesties. Shortages in church treasuries. Shortages in school funds. Shortages in community funds. Shortages at banks. Shortages — shameful. Shortages— senseless. Shortages — sinful. Because people are short on real sixteen-ounces-to-the-pound and thirty-six-inches-to-the-yard honesty.

In May, 1933, I read from a Florida paper these words: "Tagged the past week by Roland Eiby, state license inspector, were many prominent Jacksonville citizens and business men, for operating motor cars with improper licenses. Names that adorn the Blue Book — cars with eight and sixteen cylinders — were among the grist. The worst offenders against the tag law are those who can afford to buy their proper plates. We have the least trouble with the poor people."

Chauchard was a French merchant — and dishonest. He amassed millions as proprietor of a department store in which he paid notoriously low wages. When he died in Paris in 1009, he left his employees seventy-five dollars each — or a sum equivalent to that. He was wrapped in a shroud with pearl buttons —a shroud that cost one hundred thousand dollars. Grand opera singers received fabulous sums for their requiems at his funeral. He was buried in a casket that cost one hundred thousand dollars. But this post-mortem display could not erase from the minds of the people the shame of his dishonest oppression.

I am glad to believe that grand old word — "Honesty"— is going to have a glorious resurrection from the dead. It has been buried under a false entry; it shall be raised in fourfold restitution. It has been buried in the dark; it shall be raised in the light. It has been buried under evasion; it shall be raised in confession and conviction. It has been buried under broken vows, it shall be raised in remarriage with covenant keeping. It has been buried in secret; it shall be raised in the open. It has been dead under the anesthetizing of crooks; it shall be enthroned with the praise of multitudinous angels. It has been hidden in the closet with skeletons; it shall be led forth and crowned in public. It has been coffined under technicalities and subterfuges; it shall know resurrection under truth, praise and sincerity. Honesty has been stained in trickery; it shall be glorified in truth. It has been buried under the rubbish of bribery; it shall be raised clothed in splendor. It has been discarded and disowned by perjury; it shall be restored in righteousness. It has been wounded by treachery; it shall be healed under loyalty.

Some years ago — how many I do not know — I read this from the pen of Mr. S. G. Harwood of Victoria, Virginia: "Some years ago a young man on a farm decided that he would try to get into some other business. About that time a half-interest in a saw mill and manufacturing plant was to be sold. The young man and his father called to see the owners one Saturday night, and went over the proposition carefully. Before they left, they made the bargain, agreeing to pay a certain sum for this half interest in the business.

" 'You draw up the papers,' said they to the owners, 'and we will sign them and pay you the price agreed upon.'

"Sunday passed, and also Monday, Tuesday and Wednesday, the paper was not yet ready. But Wednesday night the saw mill and manufacturing plant burned down.

" 'It was lucky you and your father had not signed those papers,' remarked a neighbor to the young man Thursday morning, 'for if you had signed, you would have to pay over the money anyway.'

"The son went to his father and told him of the fire and also what the neighbor had said. The father looked at his son and said quietly, 'I have always considered my words as good as my bond.' That was all. And they paid over the sum they had agreed to pay, even though the equipment was in ruins."

Amid the loss of possessions today, and the crum-

bling of character in so many, when we think of men
like the above "we thank God and take courage."

> Lord, who shall abide in Thy tabernacle?
>   Who shall dwell in Thy holy hill?
> He that walketh uprightly, and worketh righteousness,
>   And speaketh truth in his heart;
> He that sweareth to his own hurt
>   And changeth not.

Many, I believe, even in our day, will "provide
things honest in the sight of all men" (Rom. 12: 17),
thinking on "whatsoever things are honest" (Phil. 4: 8),
"walking honestly toward them that are without" (I
Thess. 4: 12) — "providing for honest things, not only
in the sight of the Lord, but also in the sight of men"
(II Cor. 8:21). Let us, no matter how many Achans
there are to covet wedges of gold, no matter how many
Gehazis to lie about money, no matter how many
Judases to whom the jingle of money is sweeter than
the sound of music, no matter how many forsake the
honest path "just for a handful of silver, just for a
riband to stick in the coat"— let us, I say, be able
to say:

> *Pray for us: for we trust we have a good conscience,*
> *in all things willing to live honestly.*—Heb. 13: 18

Another forgotten word, so often in the discard now,
is the word

III — DO

The word "do" is quite a hobo on the highway of
life — and not everybody rejoices to have it to travel in
strength rather than to limp in impotence. Many let
the word go hungry — caring not to feed — and it has
grown emaciated and possesses a paleness which testifies to its impotence in the lives of many. It dwells

146 Glory Today for Conquest Tomorrow

among us in weakness when it should live in strength. It is given the cellar rather than the throne room in many lives. It is fed only with milk, as though it were a puny baby — instead of with strong meat as though it were a giant. We furnish it bedroom slippers, as though it were an invalid, instead of with soldier shoes of one sent forth to long marches and hard battles.

I read somewhere of how a giant and a dwarf entered into a compact to help and defend each other. So they set forth. The giant proved a poor partner and was seldom at hand when required. Seeing the dwarf alone, a wild beast fell upon him and tore off an arm. Nor did the giant put in an appearance until the dwarf had dressed his wound in such makeshift ways as he could. The giant was full of apologies and promised to do better and the dwarf readily forgave him.

On resuming the journey, the giant again fell behind and a beast of the forest attacked the dwarf and bit off a leg! The dwarf cried piteously for help, but the giant was too far behind to hear. When at length he came, as usual full of apologies, the dwarf again forgave him.

But when for the third time, the dwarf was attacked and mauled—the giant again being absent—that dwarf found energy enough to denounce a professed ally who could do nothing more than always arrive too late! Even a worm can turn and a dwarf can be indignant.

Most fine causes get a quota of supporters of the type of the giant. When there is hard work to be done, they are sure to be absent. They are much more ready to talk about the cause than to lend a hand or strike a blow. Their support is in word and name rather than deed.

There is no doubt that we put weights instead of

wings, holding-back harness instead of spurs to this great and weighty word.

Many people substitute dreams for deeds. Yet the poet, with a wisdom akin to the wisdom of the Scriptures, has written: "*Do* noble things, not dream them all day long." Many people substitute *desires* for deeds. Yet, "fulfilling the desires of the flesh" rather than the will of God, they never clothe themselves in the vigorous realities of *doing*. Many people are content to sit with a passive ambition, with their ideas never translated into deeds. Yet we have this plain injunction repeated over and over, "Whatsoever thy hand findeth to do, do it with all thy might." Many people substitute good intentions for deeds, for adequate actions. Yet they agree that not by intentions, but by *doing* do men achieve and reach forth to the realization of larger ambitions. Many people warm to glowing enthusiasm under some stirring sermon that bids us put out the fires of unworthy rest camps and forward march. Yet soon they seem to forget what James, by the Holy Spirit, wrote: "Be ye doers of the word, not hearers only, deceiving your own selves" (James 1:22). So many people plan to do, but never work the plans. They are apparently content with the blue prints rather than with the structures the blue prints call for. Their carpenter tools find unworthy rest on the blue prints. Surely they need to learn that which is written of Ezra: "For Ezra had prepared to seek the law of the Lord and *do* it" (Ezra 7:10). Many talk glibly of "surging voyages on the bounding main." Yet, with the perversity of those who bore holes in cargo ships, they are content (and comfortable) to rot in ignoble anchorage at the wharf. Surely, they need to say, with purpose and prayer, "I delight to *do* thy will, O God" (Ps. 40: 8). Jesus said: "My meat is to *do*"—not *discuss* but *do*—"the will of him that sent me and to finish his work." And it is said of Dorcas: "She was a woman full of good works and almsdeeds which she *did*." Not about which she made resolutions or had good intentions, or prayed about, but good works and almsdeeds which she *did*. And so, we have learned, and we do now know, to *do* good. But one of the greatest sins we have to deal with today is the sin of *omission*. It is not so much what many do that hurts, but what they fail to do. God had a curse placed on the people of Meroz because of the sin of do-nothingness. They did not conspire with the enemy. They did not go over to the enemy. They did not with words urge the enemy on. They just failed to help Israel in the time of trouble. It was what they did *not* do that caused the curse to be placed on them. James says:

> *Therefore to him that knoweth to do good, and doeth it not, to him it is sin.*—JAMES 4: 17

Is it not true that the sin of omission is the most costly sin that we have? Did it not cause us to lose the Eighteenth Amendment? We fought for many years— in school, in pulpit, in press, on lecture platform, in homes, in Sunday school, in prayer rooms, in temperance unions — to secure prohibition. And when we obtained it, we failed to fight to maintain it. The enemy kept on fighting for its repeal. They won. We lost — because of the sin of omission. Surely, as Isaiah would say, we need to "learn to *do* well" (Isa. 1: 17). And we have lost our Sunday night services in our churches — mainly because of the sin of omission. How we do need to recover Sunday night for God — for our God who "giveth songs in the night," for our Christ who, in the night, sweat blood in Gethsemane, after having instituted in the night the memorial supper of His broken body and shed blood. Surely we need to recall the words of the old poet:

> We live in deeds, not years,
> In thoughts, not breaths,
> In feelings, not in figures on a dial.
> He lives most who lives the best—
> Lives more in weeks than in years do some
> Where fat blood sleeps along its veins.

And surely, along with that, seeing that the fields are white already unto the harvest, we will give heed to the words of the Apostle John:

My little children, let us not love in word, neither in tongue; but in deed and in truth—I John 3: 18

And surely we need to read again the wise words of Jesus with which he closed one of His great discourses:

Not every one that saith unto me, Lord, Lord, shall enter into the kingdom of heaven: but he that doeth the will of my Father which is in heaven. . . . Therefore whosoever heareth these sayings of mine, and doeth them, I will liken him unto a wise man, which built his house upon a rock: And the rain descended, and the floods came, and the winds blew, and beat upon that house; and it fell not: for it was founded upon a rock. And everyone that heareth these sayings of mine and doeth them not, shall be likened unto a foolish man, which built his house upon the sand: And the rain descended, and the floods came, and the winds blew, and beat upon that house; and it fell: and great was the fall of it.
*—*Matt. 7: 21, 24-27

Another word listed among forgotten words is the weighty word

IV — LOYALTY

This word seems to have gone on a voyage and been lost in shipwreck, on a trip — and cannot find the way back. It is a word frequently sniffed at by scornful noses, leered at by malicious eyes, jeered at by those who loose wild tongues that hold not faithfulness in reverence. It is a word some never look up in the dictionary — use in their vocabularies, never put into rule in their lives. Vital as it is in the human makeup, it is given little place, or no place, in many lives. Many manifest no loyalty to ideals they once espoused. Many show no loyalty to their jobs. Many really do not show loyalty to friends. Many, as to their jobs, are as void of loyalty on the inside as frogs are void of feathers on the outside. Many, without loyalty to wedding hour obligations and sanctities, make perjury of their marriage vows. And we know, as we have been told by those wiser by far than we, that people who are without loyalty are as worthless and undependable as houses without foundations, as ships without rudders, as unarmed soldiers in battle, as dishes without food when the hungry are to be fed.

A columnist recently said: "Funny — even people who laugh at loyalty in a man — somehow, admire it in a dog." And a preacher recently said: "Loyalty is appreciated, admired, and praised — when found in lower animals. The dog that is loyal to his master is respected. Many dogs have shown themselves of finer quality in this regard than some people." And a newspaper editor recently wrote: "The Master asks an undivided heart, and we have no right to betray Him in the home of our friends. It is a question of loyalty. To please them would we displease Him? If so, we

are not His followers, but theirs. No man can obey
two masters. Solomon's building a heathen shrine to
oblige a heathen wife was heathenism pure and simple;
idolatry, root and branch. To neglect a duty, to compro-
mise a principle, to pull down colors, to do a little wrong
rather than to be thought a religious prig, bigoted, or,
at least, peculiar, is a great temptation; but then is the
time for the uncompromising, 'the everlasting No!' to
ring from us. Friendship that calls for disloyalty to
God needs destruction or reconstruction."

And I am sure that Dr. M. E. Dodd would have no
objections to my using here what he said on one occasion — and later wrote:

"Loyalty is one of the biggest words. It is big with
meaning. It is a red-blooded and robust word. It stands
for a big idea. It represents one of the finest qualities
of character. Loyalty is one of the noblest sentiments
with which one can be endowed. Loyalty is close kin
to royalty. One who is loyal in conduct is royal in
character. Loyalty manifests itself in every relationship of life. Loyalty, or the lack of it, may be found
between husband and wife, between parent and child,
between employer and employee, between the citizen
and his nation, between the church member and his
church, between the Christian and his Christ.

"One who regards the obligations of any relationship lightly is a light weight. Church members need to
confer with themselves often concerning the warmth and
strength of their church loyalty. If it is easy to excuse
one's self from the discharge of definite duties to the
church it is because the fires of loyalty are burning
low.

"In the long ago when God's people left Him and
His house to follow after other systems and orders, they

were called spiritual whoremongers and were said to
have been married in spiritual adultery to those whom
they followed. That is what God said in the long ago.
I do not know what He would say now about those
who give of their time, devotion and money to the
clubs, to the lodge, to the theater on Wednesday night,
or the golf links on Sunday morning, in preference
to the church of Christ.

"The Christian who is loyal to his church above all
other institutions is like the man who is loyal to his
wife above all other women, and like the patriot who
is loyal to his own flag above all other nations, and
like the child who is loyal to his own father and mother
above all other men and women."

> From over hill and plain
> There comes the signal strain,
> 'Tis loyalty, loyalty, loyalty to Christ;
> Its music rolls along,
> The hills take up the song,
> Of loyalty, loyalty, yes, loyalty to Christ.
>
> On to victory! On to victory!
> Cries our great Commander: On!
> We'll move at His command,
> We'll soon possess the land,
> Thro' loyalty, loyalty, yes, loyalty to Christ.

The motto of one of the most famous Scottish regi-
ments in the British army is "Ready, Aye Ready"!
Such is the attitude that soldiers of the Cross should
have and hold. If there is one virtue more than another
that our Lord would commend it is this very one of
loyalty — and it is never an inconsequential virtue.
To be able to stick to a task committed to us, to go on
with seeming meager results doing our job day in and
day out requires more resolute purpose than the doing

of the spectacular task that is accomplished by some brilliant spurt.

To the majority of Christ's followers has been committed only the humbler tasks requiring devotion to some obscure duty that is to be done for Him. We are like the rank and file of the army. The men who make the army are seldom heard of, but on their unswerving loyalty depends the ultimate outcome of the battles that are fought. "It is required of stewards that they be found faithful." This Jesus said. And in the final summary, this same Jesus will not ask how much praise from men we received nor how many spectacular deeds we did nor how many victories we won, but simply were we *faithful*. The rewards will be on that basis.

Another word, kin to a great host of words, that is forgotten is the word

V — UNBUYABLENESS

I do not know whether you can find that in any dictionary or not. I do not know whether you have ever used that word or not. I do not know but that the butcher blades of word mongers would chop me to pieces for saying that such a word as that should be given place in the dictionary, should be used in public address, should be utilized in conversation, should have place in any vocabulary. But if one manifests in his life what that word stands for the devil would have to yield ground, would have to surrender with regret some territory he now holds with joy. With that word in paramount position in conduct, double-crossing would be no more, being on the level always would prevail, crookedness would be a thing of the past, honor and self-respect would be maintained, and bribing would be as much in use as fur coats at the equator, or palm beach suits at the North Pole.

The devil's lie is that "every man has his price." The lie has been proved a lie by every martyr who gave his life in defense of truth since the crack of pristine dawn. A man's honor, and a woman's good name should not be, and with many, they are not for sale. To those who tried to buy Lindbergh's fame and name he said, "I don't want any more money than I am worth. I won't take any job just to capitalize my name. If I should decide to work for you, I want to be paid what I can actually earn. I'm not worth much, except my name, and I won't sell that." And that sounds like something and somebody! One is reminded of General Robert E. Lee who at the close of the war was sought by commercial enterprises for the use of his name. One concern was an insurance company and to the spokesman "Marse Robert" said: "But I know nothing about the insurance business." When it was explained to him that he hardly needed to know aught of that business as the company's directors wished only to procure the use of his name, out flashed the unforgettable answer: "My name is not for sale."

In Proverbs 22: 1, we read:

> *A good name is rather to be chosen than great riches,*
> *and loving favour rather than silver and gold.*
> —Prov. 22: 1

Men have believed that — and have acted accordingly. Dr. Herbert Adams Gibbons, in his biography of John Wanamaker, shows as much in a chapter on "Riding the Storm." "During the critical weeks of November (1907) setbacks came unexpectedly several times, despite Wanamaker's optimism. . . . He was

at his wit's end, and there were days when he confessed
to himself that he was being pushed to the wall.

"But once, when he was put to the test, he would not
admit himself beaten, although a way out was offered
him. Thinking that they could tempt him to give up
the fight, a certain group made him an offer which
seemed to be decidedly to his advantage, under the
circumstances. They announced their willingness to
buy him out, giving him a price to be set by impartial
appraisers for his buildings and stocks, and ten million
dollars in addition for the name and good-will of John
Wanamaker. Acceptance of this offer would have
enabled him to emerge from a panic a rich man; on
the other hand, its refusal, it was intimated to him,
might mean that his fortune would be swept away.
Wanamaker refused even to discuss it. Adverse circumstances might compel him to part with his buildings
and their stocks, but his name was not for sale."

The last word among forgotten words that I shall
mention is the word

VI — NOW

A positive, not a negative religion is the religion of
the Lord Jesus Christ. Not tomorrow, but today, its
duties are to be performed. Yet so many, when God
says "Now" say "tomorrow." And "tomorrow and tomorrow and tomorrow creeps in this petty pace from
day to day to the last syllable of recorded time." Some
have never learned that today is the wise man's day,
that tomorrow is the fool's day.

While undue precipitation is to be avoided, procrastination that does not include the duties of the *now* is
dangerous — dangerous for ourselves, dangerous for
others. By definite impressions God has spoken to us

at times — telling us to speak to some lost soul. We put it off until some other day. One day the message came that the person upon whose heart we should have placed the claims of Christ was dead — dying lost, and going to a Christless, churchless, musicless, Sabbathless hell. And many people who are now lost— unprepared for eternity — once heard and once felt the call to accept Christ. They put off doing it. Today they are lost. Terrible cost — the price we pay for procrastination.

Procrastination is the nation in which so many, many people live. Men who are slaves to liquor put off breaking those slave chains, postpone giving up the habit of drink. A noted surgeon once said: "If this man had had the operation two years ago, when he ought to have had it, he would have been well. By waiting he made chances against him nine to one where two years ago it was nine to one in his favor."

In moral and spiritual matters we procrastinate more easily than in material matters. Many living on disso-lution by irresolution in the face of moral duties of spiritual demands. With many, even though most of the glorious promises that shine forth like stars along the pages of the Bible are in the present tense, the new leaf that has been fingered for years is still unturned— and the attention to let God have His way is still only an intention that is gasping for breath. The *sometime* is oft never to be.

Many times, with multitudinous words, we have had the folly, the loss, the shame, the sin of delay — of not having NOW actively in our vocabularies — put upon our minds and hearts. Listen to what some men say:

Shakespeare: "Defer no time; delays have dangerous

ends. If we delay we waste our lights in vain — like lamps by day."

Carlyle: "No man has learned anything rightly until he knows and feels that every day is doomsday."

Spanish proverb: "When the fool has made up his mind, the market has gone by."

Young: "No man ever served God by doing things tomorrow. If we honor Christ, and are blessed, it is by the things which we do today."

Lavater: "The procrastinator is not only indolent and weak, but commonly false too."

"He who prorogues the honesty of today till tomorrow, will probably prorogue his tomorrow to eternity."

Cotton: "Tomorrow is a sharper who takes thy ready cash, and pays thee nought but wishes, hopes, and promises, the currency of idiots." "Tomorrow is a period nowhere to be found — unless in the fool's calendar. Wisdom disclaims the word, nor holds society with those who own it."

Southwell: "Good is best when soonest wrought; Lingering labors come to nought."

Cowper: "Doing nothing with a deal of skill."

Heriod: "The man who procrastinates struggles with ruin."

Tillotson: "To be always intending to live a new life, but never to find time to set about it — this is as if a man should put off eating and drinking and sleeping from one day and night to another, till he is starved and destroyed."

Congreve: "Delay not till tomorrow to be wise; Tomorrow's sun to thee may never rise."

Macartney: "The great opportunities of life are opportunities of today and not of tomorrow. To say tomorrow to them, as Felix did, is to say good-bye to them. To say tomorrow when God says today may mean farewell to God. Light rejected may become darkness."

With a great preacher, I say that if the stones should cry out of these walls of this building — where the Gospel has been preached as truly and as earnestly as I could preach it—and the beams out of the timber should answer them, what a history they would relate of consciences stirred, of hearts softened, of people who were almost persuaded to turn from their sinful paths and seek pardon and life eternal in Christ.

I beg you strike your tents and start for Canaan. Quit studying that road map. Start. Put out the fires of your procrastination camp. Arise and go! Maybe a thousand questions you cannot answer now. But there is one question you can settle — independent of man, independent of woman, independent of angel, independent of devil. And that is that you will be a God's man, a God's woman, henceforth and forever. Clasp hands with God — NOW. Make a league with the eternities — NOW. Accept Him with all your doubts and all your sins — NOW. Take Christ, and He will blot out all your sins — NOW. Here, at this very moment, He is waiting and pleading. Break with ignoble anchorage at Satan's wharf, and start out on the voyage of life, defying both calm and cyclone, saying with Alford:

> One who has known in storms to sail
>   I have on board;
> Above the roaring of the gale
>   I hear my Lord.
> He holds me when the billows smile;
>   I shall not fall.
> If short 'tis sharp, if long 'tis light;
>   He conquers all.